Victorian London's Middle-Class Housewife

Middle-class housewife in a contemporary outdoor dress, c. 1886.
Artwork by Jason Dunda.

Victorian London's Middle-Class Housewife

WHAT SHE DID ALL DAY

Yaffa Claire Draznin

Contributions in Women's Studies, Number 179

GREENWOOD PRESS
Westport, Connecticut • London

Library of Congress Cataloging-in-Publication Data

Draznin, Yaffa, 1922–
  Victorian London's middle-class housewife : what she did all day / Yaffa Claire Draznin.
    p. cm.—(Contributions in women's studies, ISSN 0147–104X ; no. 179)
  Includes bibliographical references and index.
  ISBN 0–313–31399–7 (alk. paper)
  1. Middle class women—England—London—History—19th century. 2. Housewives—England—London—Social conditions. 3. London (England)—Social conditions. I. Title. II. Series.
HQ1600.L6D73 2001
305.43′649′09421—dc21   99–055116

British Library Cataloguing in Publication Data is available.

Copyright © 2001 by Yaffa Claire Draznin

All rights reserved. No portion of this book may be reproduced, by any process or technique, without the express written consent of the publisher.

Library of Congress Catalog Card Number: 99–055116
ISBN: 0–313–31399–7
ISSN: 0147–104X

First published in 2001

Greenwood Press, 88 Post Road West, Westport, CT 06881
An imprint of Greenwood Publishing Group, Inc.
www.greenwood.com

Printed in the United States of America

The paper used in this book complies with the Permanent Paper Standard issued by the National Information Standards Organization (Z39.48–1984).

10 9 8 7 6 5 4 3 2 1

Contents

Preface		vii
Acknowledgments		xv
Part I	**The MCMW's Background, 1850–1875**	
1	Growing Up Female in Mid-Century England	3
2	Greater London in 1875: A Resident's View	15
3	The MCMW's Spouse and the Couple's First Home	25
4	The Matron's Appearance: Her Looks and Her Clothing	35
Part II	**The Reality: Life in Greater London, 1875–1900**	
5	The Housewife as Lowly Domestic: Cleaning the House and Doing the Laundry	47
6	The Housewife as Specialized Domestic: Preparing the Meals and Clothing the Family	59

7	The Housewife as Employer: Managing the Servants	71
8	The Housewife as Financial Manager: Balancing the Budget	81
9	The Housewife in Her Maternal Role: As Bride, Potential Mother, and Pregnant Wife	95
10	The Matron as Guardian of the Family's Health	107
11	The Matron as Nurturer of the Children: Early Child Care and Education	119
12	The Matron as Social Secretary and Activities Coordinator	129
13	The Matron as Morals Arbiter: Managing the Family's Religious and Charitable Obligations	141
14	The Matron as Her Own Person: Satisfying Personal Needs Within and Outside the Home	149
15	The Middle-Class Housewife as Shopper: The Emergence of Late-Nineteenth-Century "Consumerism"	159

Part III   The End of the Century: Conclusion

16	London in 1900: A World City Reluctant to Change	171
17	The Middle-Class Housewife in 1900: Inadvertent Agent for Change	179
	Appendix: Victorian Money	191
	Bibliography	193
	Index	205

Photo essay follows p. 106

Preface

The concept of this book, an in-depth study of a special category of British women, developed almost inadvertently. My original interest in Victorian women began when I started to research a biography (never carried through to fruition) of that extraordinary early feminist, the late-nineteenth-century, South African-born writer, Oliver Schreiner. From Schreiner, my interest segued to other late-Victorian British women and focused, as did so many of us who discovered women studies in the 1970s, on those whom I called the "notables." These were the women who, despite overwhelming pressures simply to marry, have children and embrace the cult of domesticity, broke out of the mold. They struggled to develop in a different direction, to break down the barriers of discrimination in employment, education and political participation they saw around them, to fight against the injustices and exclusions practiced against women. Their struggles engaged my attention amid an awakening sense of outrage.

But gradually, almost begrudgingly, I realized that my real interest lay, not in the notables (whose accomplishments I in no way want underrate, then or now) but in a singular group of "nonentities," women who never joined the battle at all, but spent unobtrusive lives as stay-at-home housewives in the London suburbs at the end of the nineteenth century.

At the beginning it was a simple curiosity about someone with whom I felt an extraordinary, inexplicable empathy: the ordinary Middle-Class Married Woman (whom I dubbed, with affection, "my lovely MCMW"), struggling to cope, just as I did sixty years later, with that amorphous, deceptively simple but all-consuming job of being a housewife. Confined to a house built on the vertical (steps, steps, and more steps!) with almost no labor-saving devices and only minimal household help, she devoted endless hours and an enormous amount of energy trying to reconcile fast-rising expectations of a growing family with a very limited income. Repeatedly I wondered: however did she manage to do it?

In the end, when I recognized that my quiet obsession could no longer be ignored, I had my research project encapsulated in a single, all-encompassing question: "But what did she *do* all day?"

What indeed? From this opening, other questions suggested themselves: "What was her background?" "What was the occupation and income of the man she married?" "What was London like in 1875?" "Where did she and her husband live?" "What did their house look like?" "What did *she* look like?" "How many children did the couple eventually have?" "How were the children educated?" Seeking answers to what appeared to be fairly uncomplicated questions seemed a useful research approach into an relatively unexplored field.

At the outset, it appeared evident that the Victorian housewife did far more than just the traditional chores of cleaning the house, doing the laundry, and preparing the meals. Using my own experiences as a guide, I envisioned her involved in all the family functions implicit in running a household: budgeting the family income, acting as an employer of household help, deciding when to have children and how many (was this not her choice as well as that of her husband?), coping with pregnancy and childbirth, raising the children and planning for their early education, overseeing the family's health, acting as spousal/family social secretary, undertaking various religious and charitable duties, and (later in her marriage) providing for her own growth and self-improvement.

In each of these areas, her role appeared both central and crucial. Moreover, her ability to handle such diverse functions required a certain degree of competency, considering that in a period and class that saw the beginning of the nuclear household, it had to be done with little or no maternal supervision or sisterly support. She of course had no systematic training for any of these duties.

But the simple question I initially posed proved far more profound than I realized and finding answers to the subsidiary questions far more difficult than I had imagined. As will be shown, it turned out that we really *had* no idea what the middle-class married woman did all day!

When I began my research, I gave little thought to formalized methodology since my original intention was to write a narrative that, academically sound enough to withstand scholarly scrutiny, would be understandable to an intelligent lay audience. For that reason I chose not to seek out original statistical data myself but to rely on the research of reputable historians who had done work on the British middle class of the late–nineteenth century in the income subclass and the gender of my interest. While I did not expect appreciable disagreement about the underlying data, I recognized that even experts might differ in interpretation. If this took place, I felt qualified, as a Victorian historian myself, to choose among competing interpretations, finding the perspective that corresponded most closely with my own analyses.

The parameters of the study appeared to set themselves. Since my focus was the middle-class married woman who lived in London in the last quarter of the nineteenth century, these four criteria defined a field homogeneous enough to justify generalizations and to be both "discoverable" and "scrutinizable." I chose London rather than all of urban England to represent a sufficiently large yet uniform milieu. The last quarter of the century concentrated on an area with which I was most familiar. The middle-class emphasis pinpointed the population segment emblematic of the Victorian era and, in my opinion, synonymous with change; while the occupational category of "housewife," most significant of all, embraced some 80 percent of all the women of Great Britain.

Once the place, time, social class, and "profession" of the woman was defined, I would then turn (I thought) to that huge repository of autobiographies, diaries, memoirs, and journals written by Victorian women. This documentation, I was certain, contained anecdotal details to tell me what "my" Victorian woman did all day. Although some of these works were self-excluders (e.g., written by single women, women living in an earlier period, or those in a rural rather than urban setting), what remained would be more than sufficient to reveal the lives I sought.

Finally, and only as a bit of embroidery and not for substance, I would turn to the (then) contemporary literature to give my picture literary panache, the brush of imagination to highlight the historical facts I had gathered.

Considering that the 1875–1900 time frame was comparatively recent in historical terms and the middle-class focus a familiar nineteenth-century theme, I anticipated finding more source books than I could possibly use. I couldn't have been more wrong.

I was unprepared to discover how few scholarly works scrutinized the middle class with a historical perspective through an analysis of statistical data, studying occupation and income rather than mores of behavior, expectations, and aspirations. According to historian Patricia Branca, the British middle-class has been the most understudied of all the social groups in Great Britain. In fact, Branca's work on mid–nineteenth century middle-class women, *Silent Sisterhood: Middle Class*

Women in the Victorian Home, undertook an initial analysis of the middle class as a whole and is one of the few studies that tried to quantify the material base that underlay the middle-class lifestyle, establishing the income level and the actual amount of money needed to maintain the middle-class values so amply detailed by others.

And if a dearth of research based on data characterized the picture of the Victorian middle-class population as a whole, the lack of documentation became even more striking when one tried to learn about the half that was female. Middle-class men at least earned salaries, were counted in censuses, paid taxes, and engaged in activities in the public arena: They left public records. Housewives who carried on their activities behind closed doors had no public records to leave.

These women left no records at all: This was the greatest surprise of all. I had placed great store in learning about women's domestic lives from the printed journals, diaries, autobiographies, and memoirs that Victorian women had written; but few of the hundreds of works I scrutinized, both in the original and as summarized in the reference guide, *Women in Context: Two Hundred Years of British Women Autobiographers, A Reference Guide and Reader* (compiled by Barbara Penny Kanner and others), supplied any significant information about the housewife experience. Written either by notable women or by women with the self-awareness and leisure to record the unique events of their lives, these autobiographical writings recorded, understandably, the authors' considerable public or significant achievements. They had little to say about the ordinary, routine family-related chores.

But for the housewife, the family-related chores and the house-and-family routines comprised the only life she knew or wanted. Busy with her daily duties, the housewife had neither the time nor the interest to write memoirs. In the context of the written word, she remained unknown, invisible, overlooked by history entirely.

Still I felt data must exist somewhere. Since self-revelatory sources proved only peripherally helpful, I looked to other nineteenth-century writings. One source, fiction written about middle-class Victorian women by the then-contemporary authors, seemed promising. Unfortunately (for my purposes, not enlightenment in general), it was not. I could not discover a proper "fit," that is a fictional heroine who lived in London at the end of the nineteenth century and whose middle-class husband earned a moderate income. While the outer appearances seemed analogous, the significant details (beyond descriptions of clothing or the house) were lacking.

But fiction showed me how a perceptive mind could recreate a truth—so sometimes I tried, through thoughtful speculation, to envision this woman whose life was so lacking in documentation. When no records could be found, I have on occasion combined an extensive knowledge of Victoriana with a deep familiarity with housewifery to set up a model of probable authenticity, always using the words "probably," or "likely," or "it is possible" to show that what was depicted was not a hard certainty. Insight may not be evidence but it frequently can reveal what is true.

In the end, nineteenth-century nonfiction provided the information I sought about how my lovely MCMW lived—or at least was perceived to have lived. Most useful were books written not *about* but *to* women, what we call "how-to" manuals: books on household management, health pamphlets, marriage manuals, instructional works on child care, and so forth. While these sometimes posed evaluation problems, either by being directed to women in a higher income bracket than was typical or by describing middle-class actions that the writers felt the readers *should* follow rather than what the average matron *did* follow; at least they addressed practical problems housewives faced every day. Late nineteenth-century magazines directed to matrons whose incomes fell in the middle of the middle-class range also proved useful, particularly when the editors printed letters to the editor, highlighting what the readers really wanted to know.

I also consulted works not directed toward women at all: books on the scientific, technological, and commercial advances in nineteenth-century Britain. When the subject matter in these books on urban transportation, medicine and medical practice, public sanitation and services, inventions, business practices, commercial expansions, and banks verged into the area of domestic science, infrequent though that may have been; I looked to see, and did indeed discover, how my lovely MCMW used the technology of the outside world to enrich her own.

I then perceived that, by addressing her own private needs, the middle-class matron may have inadvertently redefined those of the outside world as well.

Anonymous and private as the MCMW was, her numbers were large and her needs-soon-to-become-demands strong. By the last quarter of the century, she had begun to cast off the passivity of earlier generations, looking instead for something different, and better, than her mother had. Without any plan on how to achieve undefined goals, she knew that she wanted a more pleasant life for herself and her family. She wanted new mechanical devices to make household chores less back-breaking, more free time to spend as she wished, a simpler environment for herself and her family (including a more family-friendly house), better early care for the children, better health services for herself and her family to prevent the worries of recurring illness, more family recreation, and more products to help her lead a more indulgent life.

While these aspirations were undoubtedly held by women of other social classes, the middle-class woman apparently possessed a combination of ways and means that was unique. She had what working-class women did *not* have: the surplus income to spend beyond the necessities. However, having a disposable income alone did not make her distinctive; wealthy women had that and more. What wealthy women did *not* have was the incentive to change. Having many servants and lives of leisure, they were satisfied with things as they were; middle-class women were not.

Aware of the limitations set by her budget, the MCMW cast about for alternatives. Unable to afford the expensive labor-savings devices the wealthy had (namely servants), she opted for mechanical devices such as a home sewing machine and the Bissell carpet sweeper, and looked for even greater technological wonders in the future to free her from drudgery. When having free time became more important than just saving money, she began to buy things others had made (such as ready-to-wear clothing and prepackaged goods) rather than making them "the old-fashioned way." By her eager patronage of retail establishments where new concepts of selling stressed attention to customer needs, she indicated strong support for enterprises that catered to the consumer.

By the late nineteenth century, these women had developed into a subclass with uncoordinated but insistent goals which we today broadly identify as "consumerism." Whether the commercial marketplace—aided by the new advertising and public relations professions—began to provide customer services before they were actually expressed, or whether commerce responded to an already articulated demand by the women of the middle class is not clear. What is certain, however, is that the insistent wishes of the late-Victorian housewife dovetailed with the market's readjustment and innovation at century's end to provide a new perspective for the future.

Although my lovely MCMW had no specific social agenda, she inadvertently became one of Britain's most potent engines for change. Because change served her own ends, she made necessary and respectable the idea that change in and of itself was a good thing. In so doing, she helped forge the more positive national attitude toward modernization with which Great Britain greeted the twentieth century.

Acknowledgments

As an independent scholar with no readily available support group to provide extensive peer review, I have been fortunate in finding colleagues who provided in quality what I lacked in quantity. I gratefully acknowledge the help of two academics who have read my manuscript, offering cogent comments and much appreciated analyses: Joyce Berkman, professor of history and adjunct professor of Women's Studies at the University of Massachusetts, Amherst, and Martha Vogeler, professor emerita of English and comparative literature at California State University, Fullerton. I closely considered and incorporated many of their suggestions, while absolving them, of course, from any responsibility for what I have done on my own. I also want to thank Ozzie Badal, who read the manuscript meticulously, catching many mistakes and oversights.

In addition, let me express my gratitude to Hanna Holburn Gray, president emerita and Harry Pratt Judson Distinguished Service Professor of history at the University of Chicago, who, by sponsoring me as a visiting scholar, enabled me to obtain, among other things, the most essential tool of scholarly research—an office of my own in the library. Without it, I probably could not have completed this work.

Finally to my husband Julius, my deepest appreciation for his abiding and enveloping support of my scholarly efforts, not the least of which has been a constant financial subsidy that, as we grow older, could more profitably be spent on mutual pleasures. As he is my faithful Patron of the Arts, I am his most grateful and loving admirer.

PART I

THE MCMW'S BACKGROUND, 1850–1875

CHAPTER 1

Growing Up Female in Mid-Century England

The story begins, not in 1875 when the young lady set up residence in London as a newlywed, but twenty-five years before. To understand the woman of the 1880s and 1890s, one must know something of her background—but "know" is an elastic term. As we shall see, much of what we know about her life in mid-century and later is drawn from anecdotal and inferential evidence, supported by only sketchy documentary proof.

The third quarter of the century began, appropriately enough, with the Great Exhibition of 1851, truly the first World's Fair, at which Great Britain proudly showed off its industrial might to the world, her outstanding manufacturing preeminence being displayed in over 100,000 exhibits. It took place in a gigantic prefabricated structure of steel and glass called the Crystal Palace, originally erected in Hyde Park of London and visited by no fewer than six million people during the four and a half months it was open at that location.[1] (The Crystal Palace was set up as a more permanent structure in Sydenham in 1854; there it remained, open to the public, until it burned down in 1936.)[2]

Our young lady was born in the early 1850s, a decade that saw England's recovery from a time of great discontent and economic distress ("the hungry forties") into a thirty-year period of prosperity and relative stability. We know her birth decade because of our assumption that she married in or about 1875; according to census statistics, middle-class women married at about age 25.[3] Middle-class Victorian men often were older when they married, sometimes well into their 30s, having had to wait until their incomes were large enough to support a wife,[4] but this restraint did not apply to women. The women of the middle-class married, in fact, only one to three years later than the female population in general.[5]

We also presume, on more tentative grounds, that the young lady's parents were middle-class themselves, since the girl married a man of that class. Although there are no hard statistics on this, the prevailing middle-class conventions prescribed that marriage take place within one's own class, a union of social equals.[6] Although a family may have welcomed good fortune if their daughter married a man of the upper class, heavy scorn was reserved for daughters who married beneath their station.[7]

It is hard to determine where the young girl's father fit into the middle-class category in terms of income or occupation. Although a great deal of research has concentrated on the Victorians' middle-class values, comparatively little has been done in establishing a clear economic definition of the middle-class or in determining the specific incomes earned in the various occupations.[8] Too often, the definition of the middle-class by occupation resolved itself into a whatever-is-left-over proposition: that is, the population that lay between the agricultural or wage-earning manual workers (the floor) and those of the upper-class who derive an income primarily associated with the possession of land (the ceiling).[9]

In the eighteenth and early-nineteenth century, the middle class consisted primarily of wealthy merchants, manufacturers, bankers, and the "old" professions (Church of England clergymen, military and naval officers, those in the higher levels of law, medicine and government, university professors and headmasters of prestigious schools).[10] Later in the century it broadened to include businessmen and managers above the grade of foreman, possibly farmers who were employers, civil engineers and architects, men of the "newer" professions such as accountants, journalists, surveyors, insurance agents, and police inspectors; retail shopkeepers, clerical workers, some independent craftsmen, commercial travelers, and school teachers.[11] It is obvious that the income ranges within this category were huge.

It would have been useful if figures existed to show a correlation between middle-class occupations and income in order to determine how many people fell into each category. Unfortunately, the two official statistical sources historians traditionally rely upon for data, census returns and official tax records, had so many deficiencies in the nineteenth-century that they were unusable for this purpose.[12] However, a private study made by a nineteenth-century researcher in 1868 did show a linkage between income and occupation, revealing (in round figures) that 150,000 middle-class families had incomes of over £300 per year, some 638,000 fell into the £100–£300 a year category, and 757,000 families earned under £100 per year.[13] Thus a substantial number of middle-class families, about 42 percent of the total, lived on an income from £100 to £300 per annum.[14] If the father of the young girl of our study was "typical," he fell into this income bracket. Significantly, as will be explained later, his income permitted him to provide his wife (that is, our girl's mother) with only one servant: a maid-of-all-work.

Where was the young girl born and where did she grow up? Empirical evidence suggests that "middle-class" intimates urban living. "Country" consisted primarily of agricultural cottagers and the gentry,[15] the only village middle-class occupations being those of schoolmaster (although a village was much more likely to have had a schoolmistress), perhaps a shopkeeper, perhaps the on-site employees of the gentry. The professionals who served the cottagers, such as the doctor or the visiting clergyman, came from the nearby market town—but even the market town offered only limited middle-class employment.[16]

Population statistics show evidence of people in middle-class occupations moving to London by mid-century,[17] to become part of that city's expanding middle-class population. Because of a lack of hard data, one can only say there is a strong suggestion that the family lived in London which, by then, had become England's major commercial and business center.[18]

The girl of our study was one of many children. Victorian families in the 1850–60s averaged about six children,[19] even taking into account a high infant mortality rate (60 infants out of 1,000 died in 1870 as compared to 18.3 out of every 1,000 sixty years later).[20] About one-fifth of all families had ten or more children.[21] Because of this, the family's limited income would have been sorely stretched.

The girl's preschool upbringing would therefore have been comparatively haphazard since it is doubtful that the family could afford a nursemaid in addition to the general servant. If a nursemaid had been hired, she would also have been a maid-of-all-work, doing housecleaning along with her child-minding.[22] Most probably, the only nursemaid in the family was the mother or an older sister.

Once the young girl reached school age, her education was equally informal. Since no compulsory public education was required for children until 1870, formal education entailed the payment of fees. Educating the daughters, even if the parents felt it a good thing, depended largely on the incidence of boys in the family; whatever surplus income was available for education purposes was reserved for them. Given the family's income restraints, paying for the education of even one boy would have been enough to deprive the girls, whatever their number, of any outside schooling.

Although fiction about the nineteenth century depicts middle-class girls being taught by governesses or sent off to boarding schools, it is unlikely that this kind of education was typical.[23] The census statistics show that there were hardly enough governesses in 1851 to educate the children of the upper classes or those in upper-middle-class families, leaving none to be hired by families of more moderate incomes.[24] If the young girl was fortunate enough to live near a day school, she may have received some formal education there but never for any length of time, a year at most.[25]

However, we know the girl received a systematic education somewhere because, as a married woman, she was able to do the household accounts (requiring elementary mathematics), correspond with friends (requiring knowledge of spelling, grammar, syntax, and penmanship), and read ladies' magazines, newspapers, how-to literature, and light fiction. Most likely she was taught at home, probably by her mother[26] (although on occasion an indulgent father) or an older sister. In London, she may also have had access to books in the libraries maintained by various religious societies or the newly established, but poorly stocked, government free public libraries.[27]

Part of her education, of course, included learning the practical arts of housekeeping, which included hand sewing (and mending) and basic cooking.[28] In this income bracket, it is doubtful if learning fancy sewing or embroidery had high priority.

Since she did not go off to school, what did the girl do during the day while growing up? Surprisingly, the answer is not self-evident. Considering the size of the family and the house, one would presume that girls in middle-class families did household chores such as cleaning, doing laundry, and preparing meals. But this was not necessarily true. Middle-class mores of the mid-fifties were quite insistent that middle-class children did not do servants' work. Either the mother and the solitary maid-of-all-work did all the back-breaking labor in the house while the daughters did nothing—or else the housewife put her daughters to work at home and risked the shame that would result if friends or neighbors learned about her actions.

Presumably accommodations were made, depending on the girl's own bent and the mother's absolute need of help in the house. If the girl was interested in books at all, the mother may possibly have excused her from chores so that she could pursue a self-taught education. If the child showed interest in the more creative parts of housework, she might have been taught how to sew family clothing on the domestic sewing machine already on the British market by the late 1850s, or be allowed to help with the cooking or marketing. However, unless the family had an income larger than the demographics show, it is doubtful if she was schooled much in the "genteel" feminine accomplishments of playing the piano, singing, painting still-lifes, or doing fancy embroidery. Otherwise, barring these activities, the young girl was allowed simply to be idle.[29]

In one area, however, the girl was undoubtedly employed. She was the unpaid helper who cared for and catered to the needs of others in the family, particularly her parents and especially her father.[30] If the parents were old or ailing and other children gone, her duty was clearly to wait on them and be at their beck and call, but even if they were well, she was duty-bound, as were all the girls, to carry out their wishes; this obligation superseded any personal aspirations of her own.[31] After her parents, she owed duty and service to her brothers, even those younger than she.[32] She would be asked to take care of younger sisters as well.[33]

Any outside activity depended on the availability of a chaperone, i.e., an older adult, married cousin, or family friend: this was an absolute necessity.[34] (In wealthier families, the servants served as chaperones, but in her family none could be spared.) Accompanied by a chaperone, the girl might be permitted to help in the church or chapel or to do charitable work, such as making home visits to the needy.

Of course, in the mid-century years, she was never permitted to do paid work, even if her family could have used the additional income; to have done so would have irrevocably damaged the family's image of respectability. It simply was not done.

Mostly, oddly enough, she simply waited for life to begin—which meant, as it turned out, waiting to marry.

At some point in her teens, even before she was ready for "romance," the middle-class urban girl went through a ritualized coming-out ceremony, showing that she was no longer a child. How this was done depended on how well off her parents were. If there was money, a special party would be held or a private dance.[35] If not, the ceremony might be the simple act of putting up her hair, or lengthening her skirts, or joining the adults at the dinner table, or becoming a part of her parents' social life.[36]

As she approached marriageable age, however, the young girl's life included more and more social activities which men also attended, all arranged by her mother; she was permitted no initiative in this whatever. While middle-class families did not have a recognized ritual of contacts that the upper-middle class and the upper class did—the London "Season" so lavishly portrayed in Victorian social history and fiction—they did have comparable mechanisms, governed by family ties, shared neighborhoods, or commonality of religion or profession.[37]

In the families where the correct religious alliances were mandatory, church- and chapel-based bazaars, evening socials and outdoor excursions were held at which members of both sexes co-mingled; sometimes even simple attendance at religious services would serve as an occasion for social introductions.[38] For the families with more secular interests, theater parties, readings, concerts and dances, even seaside holidays became organized opportunities arranged for the marriageable girls to meet eligible men.[39]

Sports became an important mechanism in this process,

even embracing the momentary craze for roller skating in 1875–76.[40] Lawn tennis tournaments were especially popular, less as a sport than a social event, during which the young ladies played holding their skirts with one hand while gently hitting the ball with a racket held in the other. The men played tennis in coats and straw hats, wearing collars and ties.[41]

To avoid having their daughters tempted into making an unsatisfactory alliance, middle-class mothers tightly controlled the contacts their daughters made, expending an enormous amount of energy to make sure that the girls never met ineligible men.[42] The mother's efforts did not cease until an eligible man finally made clear his intentions to marry the young lady.

In 1875 the suitor proposed directly to the girl. Only after she accepted did he approach her father.[43] The father's role was to inquire into his prospective son-in-law's financial prospects, in order to determine how long the engagement would last.[44] Because a couple could get married only when the man's income was large enough to support a wife in the style to which she was accustomed, engagements often stretched for many years.[45]

Eventually the girl was married and, in 1875, the ceremony was comparatively simple. It often took place before the morning service at church, followed by a small family breakfast at the bride's home after the service. Afterwards, the newlyweds usually went off for a wedding trip.[46]

What the young lady did from then on for the next twenty-five years as a middle-class married woman in London now becomes the focus of our attention.

NOTES

1. Priscilla Metcalf, *Victorian London* (New York: Praeger, 1972), 56.

2. Ibid., 57–59, on the wonders of the Sydenham Crystal Palace.

3. See Table 1, "Proportions of Unmarried, Married and Widowed Females in Various Age Groups," from the *Census of England and Wales, 1911*, as reproduced in Patricia Branca, *Silent Sisterhood: Middle-Class Women in the Victorian Home* (London: Croom Helm, 1975), 3.

4. Branca, *Silent Sisterhood*, 4.

5. Ibid., 4–5.

6. F.M.L. Thompson, *The Rise of Respectable Society: A Social History of Victorian Britain, 1830–1900* (Cambridge, Mass.: Harvard University Press, 1988), 99.

7. Ibid.

8. Branca, *Silent Sisterhood*, 38.

9. Roy Lewis and Angus Maude, *The English Middle Classes* (New York: Alfred Knopf, 1950), 9.

10. Sally Mitchell, *Daily Life in Victorian England* (Westport, Conn.: Greenwood, 1996), 21.

11. Drawn up from listings in Lewis and Maude, 9; in Mitchell, *Daily Life*, 21; and in Geoffrey Crossick, ed., *The Lower Middle Class in Britain, 1870–1914.* (New York: St. Martin's Press, 1977), 12.

12. Branca, *Silent Sisterhood*, 40–41. According to Branca, because census material in the nineteenth century was not class specific, no data relating to the middle class could be pulled from the categories available. The tax returns were unreliable for other reasons: numerous tax loopholes, widespread tax evasion, and erratic compilation. So many taxpayers were omitted from their proper income categories that the use of the tax figures to determine the number in the various income brackets is highly questionable.

13. In R. D. Baxter's *National Income* (London, 1868), as quoted in Branca, *Silent Sisterhood*, 43–45. This study and another made in 1803 (Patrick Colquhoun's *A Treatise on Indigence*), both by private researchers, were regarded as accurate and of recognized validity. In making her comparison, Branca adjusted the findings to include only middle-class occupations.

14. Ibid. Though the study was made seventeen years after the MCMW of our study was born, and of the entire country rather

than just London, its findings were applicable, as Branca explains in detail.

15. Gillian Avery, *Victorian People in Life and Literature* (New York: Holt, Rinehart & Winston, 1970), 108.

16. Ibid.

17. H. J. Dyos and D. A. Reeder, "Slums and Suburbs," in *The Victorian City: Images and Realities*, H. J. Dyos and Michael Wolff, eds. (London: Routledge & Kegan Paul, 1978), 362.

18. Sally Mitchell, *Victorian Britain: An Encyclopedia* (New York: Garland, 1988), 464.

19. Thompson, *Respectable Society*, 56.

20. Alan Bott and Irene Clephane, eds., *Our Mothers: A Cavalcade in Pictures, Quotation and Description of Late Victorian Women, 1870–1900* (London: Victor Gollancz, 1932), 52.

21. Mitchell, *Daily Life*, 142.

22. Theresa McBride, " 'As the Twig Is Bent': The Victorian Nanny," in *The Victorian Family: Structure and Stresses*, Anthony S. Wohl, ed. (New York: St. Martin's Press, 1978), 49.

23. Branca, *Silent Sisterhood*, 46.

24. According to Patricia Branca, the 1871 census listed only about 55,000 governesses for the entire country; this number of governnnesses could not even have serviced the upper-class families. Moreover, with the average governess wage at £25–£45 per year, having a governess would require the family to spend from 8 to 25 percent of its annual income to retain her. Such an outlay would not have been feasible for any but the upper-middle class. From Branca's "Image and Reality: The Myth of the Idle Victorian Woman," in *Clio's Consciousness Raised: New Perspectives on the History of Women*, Mary S. Hartman and Lois Banner, eds. (New York: Harper & Row, 1974), 185.

25. Branca, *Silent Sisterhood*, 47.

26. Mitchell, *Daily Life*, 181.

27. Mitchell, *Victorian Britain*, 450–51.

28. Branca, *Silent Sisterhood*, 47.

29. In *My Days and Dreams: Being Autobiographical Notes* (London: Allen & Unwin, 1916), Edward Carpenter has a telling description of the enforced idleness of his sisters "with nothing to do and nothing to care for." It should be noted, however, that Carpenter's family had a higher income than the family in this study.

30. See Deborah Gorham, *The Victorian Girl and the Feminine Ideal* (Bloomington: Indiana University Press, 1982), for a description of the role of the daughter as consoler, comfort-giver, and general parental *helpmeet*, 38–48.
31. Ibid.
32. Ibid., 44–47; also Mitchell, *Daily Life*, 143.
33. Gorham, *The Feminine Ideal*, 20, 27.
34. Mitchell, *Daily Life*, 151.
35. Ibid., 155.
36. Ibid.
37. Thompson, *Respectable Society*, 104.
38. Ibid.
39. Ibid.
40. Esmé Wingfield-Stratford, *The Victorian Sunset* (New York: William Morrow, 1932), 227–28.
41. Ibid., 228.
42. Mitchell, *Daily Life*, 155
43. Ibid., 156.
44. Ibid.
45. Ibid.
46. Ibid., 157.

CHAPTER 2

Greater London in 1875: A Resident's View

London had grown in both area and population since the Great Exhibition of 1851, faster than any other urban area in the country and far faster than the national population as a whole.[1] Already the world's largest city by 1875, its published size varied depending on how its boundaries were defined. The county of London, which included the municipal boroughs as well as the City of London (London's 673-acre topographical and separately incorporated financial heart), was about 117 square miles in size.[2] When contiguous portions of the counties of Middlesex, Essex, Surrey and Kent ("the outer ring") were added, the total population of the Greater London metropolis was close to seven million people.[3]

Many of the 1875 landmarks were the same tourist attractions that visitors see today. Westminster Abbey, the cathedral originally founded by Edward the Confessor in the twelfth century and filled by 1875 (as now) with the statues, busts, allegorical illustrations and graves of England's notables, held regularly daily services for its parishioners. The Houses of Parliament across the road from the Abbey were rebuilt and completed in 1867 after being destroyed by fire in 1834.

Buckingham Palace, then established as the official London residence of Queen Victoria; St. Paul's Cathedral, Christopher Wren's masterpiece; the Nelson column; the refurbished Royal Opera House; Westminster Bridge (1862); the National Gallery: these and many others were all very much in use. (By the last quarter of the century, London was already an attraction for out-of-towners, indicated by the brisk sale of tourist-directed works such as *London, Past and Present* [1880], and many published photographic collections of the wonders of the city.)[4]

London already boasted many of the features one associates with a modern city. The main metropolitan railway stations of King's Cross, St. Pancras, Paddington, Charing Cross, Marylebone, Euston, and Waterloo disgorged over 300,000 men daily,[5] all coming in from the suburbs or the surrounding towns to work in the city. An underground railway system providing internal city transportation consisted at that time of three lines: the Metropolitan (first opened for service from Paddington to the City in 1863),[6] the District, and the Circle lines, the trains in the tunnels being pulled by steam-powered engines. On the surface roads, horse-drawn public omnibuses (chiefly in the hands of the London General Omnibus Company) ran on regular routes from early morning to midnight, with a number of other smaller companies running buses on irregular schedules.[7] Horse-drawn trams, whose cars ran on rails in the road, also carried commuting passengers, but these did not really become popular for the middle-class until the cars became electrified in the 1890s.[8]

Sanitary improvements, private and public, had been legally mandated for years: proper domestic plumbing (1848), pure water supplies (1852),[9] trash collection,[10] and sewage drainage and disposal (1866),[11] this last involving 1,300 miles of sewage pipes stretching beneath the city.[12] The major streets were well-lit by gas and in Holborn, electric street lighting had been installed as an experimental venture.[13]

The telegraph, run by the General Post Office (GPO), was

a fast and regularly used means of information transmission. Quick and inexpensive (twelve words for sixpence), a telegram's arrival by personal delivery was guaranteed day and night.[14] And, harbinger of things to come, the first telephone exchange run by the United Telephone Company, a private company, would open up on Lombard Street in 1879,[15] with the GPO taking over the operation the following year.[16]

Mail delivery was (compared to present-day service) unbelievably frequent, reliable, and inexpensive. In London proper, there were eight postal districts; and within the limits of the main Eastern Central district, there were twelve deliveries daily, nine of which were made to each district hourly. To the other town districts within three miles of the GPO, eleven deliveries a day were made. The remaining suburban districts received six deliveries daily.[17] It cost a ha'penny to send a postcard and only a penny postage stamp to send a letter of one-half ounce or less anywhere in England, Scotland, and Wales.[18]

But while these amenities made London a good place to work, visit, or carry on business, the city had many drawbacks that made it less attractive as a place to live.

One of the more unpleasant features of London was the extremely heavy street traffic. Horse-drawn iron-wheeled conveyances of every description jammed the roads in an unending and noisy parade, either coming in from the country or moved out into the city from trains terminals and docks. Horse-powered drays were also on the streets, transporting heavy goods between firms, while smaller horse-drawn delivery vehicles carried goods between homes, offices, businesses, shops and governmental agencies throughout the metropolitan area. By the end of the century, according to one researcher, commercial vans, wagons, carts and drays must have amounted to close to a half million vehicles; and although the proportion of these driving around London is not known, "it was [certainly] enough to overload the road system."[19]

Adding to the confusion was the profusion of conveyances

for carrying people. These carriages, all descendants from the coach, had various names and descriptions. Besides the privately owned broughams (light, enclosed, one-horse carriages)[20] belonging to individuals for their personal use, there were hackney coaches for hire, with two facing benches inside, an elevated seat in front outside for the driver, and additional room for luggage at the rear.[21] The popular Victorian taxi was the hansom cab, two-wheeled and lightweight, for carrying two or three individuals who sat with an unobstructed view of the street before them, its driver sitting on an outside elevated seat in the rear and speaking to the passengers below through a trap door.[22] (Hansom cabs were licensed and the fares more or less standardized at sixpence per mile,[23] and in many places throughout the city cabmen's shelters were erected to allow the drivers to warm themselves and get a cup of coffee.)[24]

All the vehicles on the street were drawn by living horses; that meant horse droppings everywhere.

One cannot appreciate the amount of manure on the streets by looking at Victorian photos of ragamuffin boys diligently sweeping the crosswalks to allow ladies with long skirts to walk across without getting dirty. Contemporary experts have estimated that the amount of droppings which one horse, on normal feeding and with a normal work load, produced in a year was in the range of 6 to 7½ tons.[25] As a researcher in this field commented dryly, "cumulatively the amount could be rather more than simply a messy embarrassment." An estimate was made that, by the 1830s, English towns had to cope with something like 3 million tons of droppings each year; by 1900 the figure was more like 10 million tons.

All of the muck had to be disposed of. While theoretically this manure was a valuable source of fertilizer for farmers, getting it out of the city and onto their lands posed an almost insurmountable problem. Even in towns adjacent to farming areas, a high proportion of horse droppings never was recovered by the farmers; instead, it piled up, as vast dung heaps, on scraps of waste land in the poorer sections of towns. In London, with its vastly larger horse population, disposal problems were enormous, compounded by the fact that cleaning-up operations could only be carried out at night, since squads could not shovel away the dung in the daytime without causing enormous traffic jams. And while the introduction of hard, smooth surfaced streets and curbside runoff drains did help improve the street cleaning throughout the Victorian period, it was unquestionable, in the opinion of that researcher, that the coming of the motor vehicle at the turn of the century immeasurably raised the quality of urban life by driving the smell and the squelch off the streets.

In addition to the congestion and the smell, the constant, often deafening noise of traffic was shockingly obtrusive to strangers and objectionable even to residents; those living on the main thoroughfares complained that the rumble of traffic was so loud it drowned out their dinner-time conversation. Because no one actually measured the decibel level of clattering metal-shoed hooves and iron-rimmed wheels along the cobblestone or granite streets, we have no idea of the degree of street noise of the late Victorian years; but "the possibility that the motor car made our streets quieter as well as cleaner should not be ignored."

Another major city problem and health hazard was air pollution. In 1875, food was cooked and homes were heated by coal, the soot and noxious gases pouring out into the air daily from the hundred thousand chimneys of the city causing respiratory illnesses of every sort.[26] When the gases and soot particulates combined with discharges from the Essex and Kentish marshes during the winter, the result was an almost impenetrable fog, the proverbial "peasouper" of fact and fiction. One of the handbooks on the city described a "London particular" (as it was also called) as follows:

Not only does a strange and worse than Cimmerian darkness hide familiar landmarks from the sight, but the taste and sense of smell are offended by an unhallowed compound of flavours, and all things become greasy and clammy to the touch. During the continuance of a real London fog—which may be black, or grey, or more probably orange-coloured—the happiest man is he who can stay at home.[27]

Far from being just romantic backdrops to Arthur Conan Doyle's mysteries, the fogs were often deadly. In what was called the Great Fog of 1886, the mortality rate rose to that of the worst cholera years[28]; and during the particularly lethal winter of 1879–1880, 2,400 fatalities were attributed to the fog.[29]

Still, it is not known whether most Londoners thought the level of municipal pollution unbearable. The poor in the slums tolerated it as they did all other negative aspects of city living. The middle-class men, subjected to it daily, may privately have deplored the odor and inconvenience but possibly held the prevalent view that noise, grime, and smells were the relatively unimportant side effects of London's bustling commercial activity, prime indicators of a healthy economy. The wealthier middle-class and upper-class women, spared the daily descent into the urban pollution that their husbands encountered, found consolation in the well-kept parks and squares with trees and greenery scattered strategically throughout the city and suburbs. However, since the pollution was also found to some degree in the suburbs where they lived, they also voiced complaints about the annoyance it caused.

The one who probably found the pollution most intolerable was the middle-class housewife who, with her single servant, had to do the physical work necessary for keeping the house and the family clothing clean. The muck, tracked onto the rugs in the house from the street and the sticky soot in the air ("the blacks") which settled on every object in her home, turning newly laundered clothes into gray shrouds by the end of the day, probably made the achievement of even a modicum of cleanliness a constant battle.

Bedeviled by this all, the now-married woman probably did all she could to persuade her new husband to move out to the suburbs. In all likelihood, he was perfectly amenable to her suggestions. Since all outlying communities were now served by a network of railway and underground lines that provided rapid transportation to and from the city,[30] the man saw no inconvenience at the prospect of moving out of London proper, and considerable advantage.

Londoners had already begun to move out of the city to the suburbs by the 1860s, following the speculative builders and real estate developers who, for over half a century or more, had been building terrace housing and villas in a series of wave-like movements away from the city.[31] The suburbs, that is, the residential neighborhoods outside of the traditional municipal districts, were places where the family could indulge in a semi-rural existence, with greenery and small gardens adjacent to their houses.[32] Each suburb was self-contained; beside the terraces or semi-detached homes, each had shops of various kinds and housed doctors and solicitors, schools, churches and chapels, and all the services of a miniature city with the exception that they had no separate newspapers.[33] (But with all their pleasantness, the suburbs still contained enclaves of huddled slums, defective sewage systems, and roads covered with horse droppings, just as in London itself[34]; and these liabilities prevailed almost to the twentieth century.)

The most important decision the couple had to make when looking to move to the suburbs was to find the suburb that suited them best. Each suburb had a character of its own, made up of a specific occupation grouping of known social status. For the greater part of the nineteenth century, London and its suburbs were segregated into neighborhoods that were almost exclusively single economic and occupational entities.[35]

Each middle-class family in any particular suburb was of an occupation and income similar to all others in that suburb; and the newlyweds looked for the suburb that best fit their income and perceived status.

By 1875, the character of many suburbs was already established. Dalston, Brixton, New Cross, Forest Hill, Walthamstow, and Tottenham were almost wholly peopled by clerks of the lower middle class.[36] Kennington, Stockwell, and Camberwell contained a large number of city tradesmen.[37] Pimlico and Paddington, once very fashionable areas, had come down in the last quarter of the century to become middle-class areas of suburban gentility.[38] Hackney, a desirable suburb with semi-detached villas and terraces, was also a "good address" until the end of the century.[39] For the man employed in the West End as a higher-paid clerk, Hammersmith with its semi-detached villas was a good choice; if he were in a somewhat higher income bracket, the suburb would be Kensington, where managerial and professional people lived with well-paid civil servants and administrators.[40] Hampstead and St. John's Wood were where doctors, lawyers, and artists lived; these were not aristocratic neighborhoods but considerably above the ordinary middle-class suburbs.[41]

Probably with the exception of Kensington, Hampstead, and St. John's Wood, the couple could have found affordable housing in any of these suburbs. In fact, by the time they married, they may already have decided upon the suburb that would be most congenial. Otherwise, by talking to friends and by canvassing the neighborhoods, they would search out the one to their liking. Not until they decided on the precise location that suited their station would they begin the serious matter of house-hunting.

NOTES

1. Asa Briggs, *Victorian Cities* (New York: Harper Colophon Books, 1970), 312.

2. *Encyclopedia Britannica*, 11th ed., vol. 16 (1911), 938. Besides the City of London, the municipal boroughs were: Battersea, Bermondsey, Bethnal Green, Camberwell, Chelsea, City of Westminster, Deptford, Finbury, Fulham, Greenwich, Hammersmith, Hampstead, Holborn, Islington, Kensington, Lambeth, Lewisham, Marylebone, Paddington, Poplar, St. Pancras, Shoreditch, Southwark, Stepney, Stoke Newington, Wandsworth, and Woolwich.

3. Ibid.

4. Mitchell, *Victorian Britain*, 465.

5. Walter Besant, *London in the Nineteenth Century* (New York: Garland, 1985), 28. This number was true in 1860. Besant had no precise number for 1875, although he estimated that, in the first decade of the twentieth century, it was 400,000.

6. Nicholas Bentley, *The Victorian Scene: A Picture Book of the Period, 1837–1901* (London: Weidenfeld & Nicolson, 1968), 256.

7. *Dickens's Dictionary of London, 1880: An Unconventional Handbook* (London: Charles Dickens, 1880), 184.

8. Bentley, *The Victorian Scene*, 255–56.

9. Mitchell, *Victorian Britain*, 465.

10. Mitchell, *Daily Life*, 80. The Public Health Act of 1875 required that municipalities collect trash and garbage on a regular basis.

11. Mitchell, *Victorian Britain*, 269.

12. Ibid., 608.

13. Michael Harrison, *The London of Sherlock Holmes* (London: David & Charles Black, 1975), 49. Also, R. D. Blumenfeld, in *R.D.B.'s Diary, 1887–1914* (London: Heinemann, 1930), 1, speaks of Holborn's experimental effort at electrical street lighting in 1887.

14. *Dickens's Dictionary*, 216–17.

15. Arthur B. Allen, *Victorian England, 1850–1900: The Complete Background Book* (London: Rockliff, 1956), 184.

16. Mitchell, *Victorian Britain*, 788.

17. *Dickens's Dictionary*, 216–17.

18. Mitchell, *Daily Life*, 83.

19. F.M.I. Thompson, *Victorian England: The Horse-Drawn Society* (London: University of London Press, 1970), 12.

20. Mitchell, *Daily Life*, 129.

21. Ibid., 75.

22. Ellison Hawks, *The Romance of Transport* (New York: Thomas Crowell, 1931), 90–91; also Mitchell, *Daily Life*, 75.
23. Mitchell, *Victorian Britain*, 812–13.
24. Metcalf, *Victorian London*, 139.
25. Thompson, *Horse-Drawn Society*, 10. All the information and quotations in this and the following two paragraphs regarding horse droppings and traffic noise are from this work, 10–11.
26. Mitchell, *Victorian Britain*, 269.
27. *Dickens's Dictionary*, 113.
28. From the "Forty-ninth Annual Report of the Registrar-General, for 1886," as reported in Anthony S. Wohl, *Endangered Lives: Public Health in Victorian Britain* (Cambridge, Mass.: Harvard University Press, 1983), 213.
29. Mitchell, *Victorian Britain*, 269.
30. Donald J. Olsen, *The Growth of Victorian London* (New York: Holmes & Meier, 1976), 314–15.
31. Thompson, *Respectable Society*, 174.
32. Mitchell, *Victorian Britain*, 767.
33. Besant, *London in the Nineteenth Century*, 29.
34. Gavin Weightman and Steve Humphries, *The Making of Modern London, 1815–1914* (London: Sidgwick & Jackson, 1983), 129.
35. Thompson, *Respectable Society*, 173.
36. In Besant, *London in the Nineteenth Century*, a caption to a photograph from Leonora Collins, *London in the Nineties*, 19.
37. Ibid.
38. Weightman and Humphries, *Making of Modern London*, 65–66.
39. Ibid., 144.
40. Ibid., 68.
41. Ibid., 32.

CHAPTER 3

The MCMW's Spouse and the Couple's First Home

It is impossible to generalize about the middle-class woman's husband in any respect. In appearance, we can only know that he probably was older than his wife and tended to facial hair. With regard to his health, we can infer that he was probably physically fit since, coming from a middle-class family without a carriage at its disposal, he must have done an enormous amount of walking through to young adulthood. In addition, if any credence can be had in the advice given in an 1888 marriage manual to young unmarried women concerned about the health of their prospective husbands; consumption (i.e., tuberculosis) and having a sexually transmittable disease (shocking thought indeed!) were among the possible health hazards.[1]

Least of all can we generalize about the man's character, relevant though it may have been to the way the housewife spent her day or managed the house. While some husbands assuredly drank or gambled, spent money irresponsibly, or perhaps even abused their wives, diminishing the women's ability to cope, others with benign natures and a sense of responsibility enabled their wives to carry out their marital duties without stress: both of these and all variations in between were possibilities.

But we *can* look profitably at the husband in an economic sense because knowing his occupation and income gives us the material parameters of the life upon which the couple was about to embark. Like the girl's father, he was a Londoner of moderate income, earning between £100 and £300 a year, the typical average income for the urban middle-class in 1875.[2] At this level, his occupation could have been any one in a spectrum: a self-employed professional of modest rank, a school teacher, a salaried public servant, a salaried clerk or shop foreman in private enterprise, a small businessman himself with a few employees of his own, a commercial traveler, or an agent or dealer who bought or sold various products.[3] The income he earned was adequate enough for him to marry but not large enough for extravagances of any kind. When he and his wife finally moved into a home of their own, his salary was large enough (at the start) to permit his wife to hire only one live-in servant or, at the most, two.

House-hunting was the first activity the married couple would do together (presuming that the husband had not already taken care of this before the marriage). While the mistress was most concerned about the house's layout, landscaping, and adaptability for living, the husband was more concerned with the suitability of the house's location and, of course, details of its construction. Since a large amount of money would be required should subsequent alteration become necessary, its structure and amenities required his closest attention.

The house was leased, not bought, a practice followed by the vast majority of British house-dwellers; owner-occupancy did not signify any particular social position nor did tenancy in itself carry any particularly social connotation.[4] (It is commonly held that only 10 percent of all pre-1914 houses in Great Britain were owner-occupied.)[5] Typically, middle-class tenants rented their houses for a fixed term of years on repairing leases that obligated them to tend to the maintenance themselves once the house was rented.[6]

The matter of layout inside the house was of only minimal concern since very little variation existed in the homes they visited; suburban houses were not built to individual tastes. All used the same floor plan established years before by builders or estate owners, with no variation to allow for individualized tenant requirements.[7]

Although rents varied somewhat from suburb to suburb, rent was a relatively small portion of a family's budget, only one-tenth or at the very most one-eighth of the husband's income[8] (as compared to the 25 to 35 percent amount allocated in a modern budget). For that amount, a wide range of choices were available, depending on location (how close or far from the High Street), the architectural style, and even the size, since houses varied in the number of rooms or stories to match the different phases of family life.[9]

The structure of the house was standard. Typically it was either part of a terrace (homes built in a row with common walls, windows only in front and back) or semi-detached (sharing a common wall with only one other home, although the separation from the house on the other side would have been small). Fully detached homes were available only in the more fashionable and expensive neighborhoods.[10] The houses were on small-width lots, narrow but tall, two or three stories high (or more) plus basement and attic, each floor consisting of a number of rooms, all fairly small.[11]

Most household advice manuals directed to the middle-class couple were replete with suggestions on what to look for when renting a home.[12] Mrs. Isabella Beeton's book contained a section on "Choosing a House" that included advice to prospective tenants on what to demand of the owner should any deficiencies be found.[13] But because houses were rented rather than sold, most owners had no reason to put in quality fixtures at the beginning and little incentive to upgrade them or the plumbing, heating, or lighting systems from what had been in place when the home was built.[14] It is not likely that the couple had any leverage to demand major owner improvements.

Most advice given in the household manuals was of only limited value. Some tips given were self-evident, such as avoiding localities with offensive odors or houses too close to noisy businesses.[15] Others, though certainly important (such as hiring a competent surveyor to inspect for proper drainage, good ventilation, and a pure water supply before signing the lease), were too expensive for a family on a limited budget to follow.[16]

In general, the houses offered for rent were defective in one manner or another, although in some cases deficient technology was to blame. Gas lighting in homes built before 1875 was usually inadequate because the jets burned with a smelly flame and used large quantities of oxygen without giving off much light; the Welsbach gas mantle improvement was not yet on the market.[17] In many rooms there were no gas fixtures at all, it being expected that the public rooms would use kerosene or oil lamps, the sleeping rooms routinely lit by candle.[18] Heating was provided by a wood- and coal-burning fireplace in every room,[19] but because fireplaces were not very efficient room warmers, renters in the 1880s sometimes placed venting flues into their fireplaces to cast the heat out into the room rather than have it be lost up the chimney.[20] In the kitchen, the owner-installed coal-burning cooking range (one item of furniture the renter did not have to buy) was seldom a late model and could even have been so old that the baking chamber was still only an oven box backed up against the open fireplace.[21]

While suburban homes already had lead pipe plumbing by 1875,[22] with faucets in the sinks and drains in the sinks or floors, the water in even these homes was ordinarily piped in only at the basement level. The water in the pipes, of course, was cold; in homes already constructed in 1875, special tanks for heating and storing hot water were not yet installed.

The renter had to make his own arrangement to get water piped into the home; nowhere in the London area was water supplied by the municipality. Each house had a separate water cistern which had to be regularly filled by a private water company with which the individual homeowner signed a contract.[23] Although the companies were required by law to keep cisterns filled on a 24-hour basis, the law was not well enforced.

Ordinarily if renters found major structural deficiencies in the house, they either had to reject the house (having no power to force the owner to add what they felt necessary) or else rent it as it was and install needed improvements at their own expense.

The inside layout of all houses for the middle class was standard. The kitchen was in the basement, together with pantries and larders.[24] In the back of the basement were the scullery, storage areas, and laundry rooms. Outside in front, an open area space admitted light and air into the basement,[25] with a flight of stairs for tradesmen to get to the basement kitchen door. In the front wall of the area was a door leading to the coal cellar under the front sidewalk where a covered coal hole on the sidewalk proved a place for coal to be delivered. In the rear, an area opened onto a tiny grassy back yard.

In the front of the house, a flight of outside stairs led up to the door on the ground floor (the American first floor); inside was an entry hall and the door to the dining room, in the front of the house. In the rear of that floor was a room for the man of the house: his library, study, or office.

The first floor (the next floor above) contained the drawing room which was, in effect, the mistress's room. It often occupied the entire floor, although sometimes the area was divided into two or three rooms by folding doors. The floor above housed the master bedroom in the front with another room in the back. (After children were born, this back room sometimes became the day nursery.)

If the house had another story, it would later house the

nursery where the children and their nursemaid, if they had one, slept, ate, studied, and played. Any other rooms on this floor became extra bedrooms or store rooms. In the attic itself were still more storage rooms and the sleeping room for the servant. All floors were connected by both front and back stairs.

All houses were rented unfurnished except that the kitchen range and possibly the table in the kitchen were supplied by the owner.[26] The public rooms (dining room, sitting room, den, and drawing room) were often wallpapered by the owner as well, though usually in a dark hue.[27] According to Mrs. Beeton, should the owner offer to repaper for the incoming tenant (as he sometimes did), the renters were to insist on seeing not only the patterns in the traditional sample books but designs "of the best known and most artistic firms."[28] (It is doubtful whether the newlyweds in this instance would have demanded this privilege.)

Once the house was rented, the couple then proceeded to choose the furniture. This was done jointly by both the housewife and her spouse, more because of the expense involved rather than any difference in taste.

It is hard for moderns to be objective in judging the furniture of this period. Descriptions of the massive, dark, and over-ornamented pieces that dominated the Victorian home even as late as the last quarter of the nineteenth century have so often been caricaturized rather than described that one tends to lean backward and try to see them as "handsome" or even "pleasing." Young people today would probably have found them neither. But the furniture the newlywed couple bought to fill up their first home would have represented to them a standard of durable excellence, tradition, and stability from which they derived great pleasure.

The furniture was not bought by the piece but as suites, that is, a series of matching pieces for each room. In the main, shopping was done by going through "pattern books" (similar to present-day mail-order catalogues) put out by various manufacturers, filled with pictures of furniture in a variety of styles, woods, decorative carving, metalwork, and upholstery to suit a broad range of tastes and incomes.[29] On occasion, the two of them might look for individual pieces on Tottenham Court Road, which, with its continuation as Hampstead Road, contained most of the established furniture shops.[30] The style most frequently featured was Gothic, the so-called British style.[31]

The suite in the parlor, the room in which the family spent most its time together, was of dark wood: mahogany, darkened oak, rosewood, or black walnut, copiously decorated with carvings in high relief.[32] The settees, overstuffed chairs and tables would eventually be covered with cloth pieces, either as decorative skirts or to protect the arms and headrests of the chairs from soil, as fashion decreed.[33] Though heavy, the best of the furniture, according to a reluctant critic, was well made, probably as good as the finest cabinet work of the Georgian period.[34]

The dining room, long and high-ceilinged, often papered in a dark crimson with heavy curtains to match, contained a table of mahogany, dark and deeply varnished, with chairs carved in the same massive style. There would be a large sideboard and, opposite it, an ornate mantle shelf, full of ornaments, with a marble clock in the middle and a large mirror behind.[35]

The rooms were generally furnished to reflect their intended use, with furniture in the drawing room and the boudoir lighter in color and more delicate than furniture placed in the library or study.[36]

A typical bedroom suite advertised by a London firm consisted of a wardrobe with plate-glass doors, a washstand with a marble top, a toilet table, a large chest of drawers, toilet glass (a mirror), three chairs, a pedestal cupboard, and a toilet airer (commode for the chamber pot).[37] The double bed was not included in the suite[38]; this was bought separately.

In 1875, the house probably did not have a separate wash

room containing a bathtub and sink or a room containing a flushing toilet, although these conveniences were already installed in the homes of the monied classes. Although a somewhat odorous water closet with working parts and flushing water had been in use by the end of the eighteenth century, an acceptable domestic toilet with its working parts in a wooden box (the "National" of Thomas Twyford) did not become a popular selling item of domestic plumbing until the decade of 1880s.[39]

Not much thought was given to the decor or furnishings of the room where the servant slept; the furniture consisted usually of cast-offs and of the most functional sort.[40]

What was not yet evident, but would begin shortly after the couple moved in, was the accumulation of accessories and furnishings that filled up every room of the house. Year after year the accumulation would go on and on giving a new definition to the word "clutter," an indulgence even housewives under the tightest budgets exercised. Below is a description one writer gave of only some of the contents of an average Victorian drawing room of the seventies and eighties, large furniture pieces excluded:

> Stuffed birds, wax flowers under glass domes, occasional tables loaded with albums containing family photographs, chairs of every size . . . stools and firescreens painstakingly worked in petit point or embroidered patchwork; cabinets, what-nots, fancy shelves supported by fancy brackets all loaded with china vases and mementoes . . . walls covered with willow patterned plates and dishes, reproductions of Sir Edwin Landsmeer's stags or Sir Frederick Leighton's Greek beauties, chromolithographs of the Alps, and such family portraits as had not already found a place on piano or mantelpiece, or in an album.[41]

Of course, the decision the newlyweds finally made to rent the house they did was not irrevocable. During the next twenty-five years, the middle-class family would move a number of times,[42] partly to accommodate their growing family but also to get into a better neighborhood as the husband rose in rank (and salary, presumably) within his company or profession. This couple's first home of choice was what newly marrieds in America today would call "a starter home." They would go on from there.

NOTES

1. Henry Arthur Allbutt, *The Wife's Handbook: How a Woman Should Order Herself During Pregnancy, in the Lying-in Room, and After Delivery . . . and Other Matters of Importance Necessary to be Known by Married Women*, 7th ed. (London: R. Forder, 1888), 56–57.
2. See explication of this in Chapter 1.
3. Geoffrey Crossick, "The Emergence of the Lower Middle Class in Britain," in *The Lower Middle Class in Britain, 1870–1914*, Geoffrey Crossick, ed. (New York: St. Martin's Press, 1977) 12.
4. Thompson, *Respectable Society*, 168.
5. Ibid.
6. Ibid., 169.
7. Olsen, *The Growth of Victorian London*, 211; also Thompson, *Respectable Society*, 168.
8. Thompson, *Respectable Society*, 172.
9. Ibid., 170, 172.
10. Ibid., 174.
11. Laura Wilson, *Daily Life in a Victorian House* (London: Breslich & Foss, 1993), 10.
12. Mitchell, *Victorian Britain*, 6–7. The most famous of these manuals was Isabella Mary Beeton's *Book of Home Management [and] a Guide to Cookery in All Branches* (London: Ward, Lock & Co.), originally published in 1861, it went into many subsequent editions, consulted well into the twentieth century.
13. Beeton, *Book of Household Management*, 27–30. This and all subsequent references are to the 1909 edition unless specifically noted otherwise.
14. Leonore Davidoff, *The Best Circles: Society Etiquette and the Season* (London: Croom Helm, 1973), 85.

15. Beeton, *Book of Household Management*, 30.

16. Ibid. This advice was also given in Elizabeth Blackwell's *How to Keep a Household in Health* (London: W. W. Head, 1870), 16–17.

17. Mitchell, *Victorian Britain*, 452.

18. Caroline Davidson, *A Woman's Work Is Never Done: A History of Housework in the British Isles, 1650–1950* (London: Chatto & Windus, 1982), 109, 112.

19. Ibid., 50.

20. John Gloag, *Victorian Comfort: A Social History of Design from 1830–1900* (London: Adam & Charles Black, 1961), 113.

21. Beeton, *Book of Household Management*, 43–44.

22. Thompson, *Respectable Society*, 193.

23. Besant, *London in the Nineteenth Century*, 373.

24. Wilson, *Life in a Victorian House*, 10.

25. Mitchell, *Daily Life*, 109. Descriptions of the house in this and the next three paragraphs are all from this source.

26. H. C. Davidson, ed., *The Book of the Home: A Practical Guide to Household Management*, vol. 1 (London: Gresham, 1905), 50.

27. Beeton, *Book of Household Management*, 28.

28. Ibid.

29. Mitchell, *Victorian Britain*, 368–69.

30. Harrison, *London of Sherlock Holmes*, 209.

31. Mitchell, *Victorian Britain*, 368.

32. Gloag, *Victorian Comfort*, 40–41.

33. Bott and Clephane, *Our Mothers*, 61.

34. Gloag, *Victorian Comfort*, 42.

35. W. Macqueen-Pope, *Twenty Shillings in the Pound* (London: Hutchinson, 1951), 207.

36. Thompson, *Respectable Society*, 176.

37. Bott and Clephane, *Our Mothers*, 63.

38. Ibid. See also illustration in Gloag, *Victorian Comfort*, 37.

39. Mitchell, *Victorian Britain*, 607.

40. Ibid., 368–69.

41. Bott and Clephane, *Our Mothers*, 63.

42. Thompson, *Respectable Society*, 171.

CHAPTER 4

The Matron's Appearance: Her Looks and Her Clothing

What then did this newly married woman look like? Women coming in many sizes, shapes and forms, it is hard to generalize with any accuracy. If we draw upon what we know about men then and now, she was probably shorter than women are today; being only five feet tall was not unusual (Queen Victoria herself was barely that).[1] As far as weight and shape were concerned, we cannot be sure. Judging from illustrations and photographs in the (then) current press, the Victorian woman in 1875 appeared to be of fairly ample proportions, with a well-developed bust, a small waist, and full hips. However, a woman's natural shape was hard to determine since the fashion of clothing did its best to alter the figure to conform to the norm that society, and she, found most attractive.

We do not know much about the general health of the Victorian woman either,[2] despite the recurring picture of the delicate maiden swooning on a sofa as a staple in early-nineteenth century literature. By the last quarter of the century, if the woman swooned with any regularity, it was because she was seriously ill, tuberculosis (known as consumption) being a major killer of women.[3] While in a later chapter the middle-class matron's health is discussed in greater detail, one might assume that, barring specific illnesses, her general health was fairly good for the same reason that we gave for men; despite a diet heavy in starches and fats and notoriously lacking in fresh vegetables and fruit, she too did a great deal of walking in childhood and adolescence.

Her appearance of beauty, comely enough in early adulthood to have brought forth a proposal of marriage, probably owed a great deal to copious advice on how to make the best of her figure, hair, and complexion, not only from her mother, older sisters and friends but from writers of articles in the many women's magazines devoted to matters of beauty and grooming.[4]

The home manuals which her mother assuredly stocked were replete with similar advice. The *Ward & Lock's Home Book: A Domestic Encyclopedia* (published as a companion volume to Mrs. Beeton's *Book of Household Management*) devoted no fewer than seventy-five pages to "The Toilet," that is, the care of the female features and figure, with many suggestions on what a woman must do to enhance her beauty.

In 1875, a woman still wore her hair long, either piled up on her head and kept in place by innumerable hair pins or as a bun low on the neck.[5] By frequent brushing and the use of curling irons or night-time curlers, women were encouraged to keep their hair curly and pliable. (The *Ward & Lock* manual also contained advice on how to crimp one's hair, on the use of false hair, on permissible "touch-up" dying, and even on the use of depilatories for the removal of unwanted hair.)[6]

Contrary to popular opinion, Victorian women *did* use cosmetics, although face powders were confined to natural products such as powdered starch or flour of oatmeal.[7] While lip coloring and rouge were not worn in public and no household manual could properly give advice on such an unacceptable subject, writers sometimes did explain, just in case a young lady had to know this "for theatrical purposes," how one might create red make-up for the lips (to cold cream with wax melted in it, add a few drachmas of carmine).[8] Advice on eye make-up was also given, including the use of various natural products to apply to the brows and around the eyes to accentuate their color and shape.[9]

Late-Victorian women were encouraged to buy commercial toiletries offered under various brand names. They, in fact, became the first large group of consumers to patronize what would become the cosmetics industry.[10] One advertisement, for example, touted a new "Parisian Vaporizor," said to provide a smooth complexion; another claimed that "Beethan's Glyceran and Cucumber Lotion," guaranteed a more youthful appearance.[11] Kalydor (an "Oriental botanical preparation") could be used to treat skin redness and pimples, Bridal Bouquet Bloom was "to beautify the complexion," and other preparations with exotic names like Aethereal Oleine, Elmes's Arcanum, Winn's Anticardium, Olden's Eukeirogenion, and Rypophagon Soap were heavily advertised as beauty enhancers.[12] Middle-class women even knew about the product called bullock's gall, ordinarily used as a cleaning product for marble, which was said to be used occasionally by the personal maids of the wealthy to remove black spots and freckles from their mistresses' complexions.[13]

It is very difficult to describe the clothing of a Victorian young lady "in general terms," not only because dresses were so elaborate but because fashions varied not only from year to year but from season to season. Styles that disappeared as the years passed reappeared as "something new" in succeeding decades. For example, crinolines, those bell-shaped cages that fit beneath a woman's skirt, enclosing her from waist to the floor, had disappeared entirely by the late 1860s; then at the beginnings of the eighties they made a modified return as the "crinolette," a half-cage-type undergarment. However, the resurrected garment's popularity was short-lived when a revolt against it, instigated by William Morris, took place among young girls who signed petitions in protest, contributing to its demise.[14] Similarly, the bustle, a pad or cushion sewn into the back of the skirt that jutted out from the body like a shelf, which had come and gone by 1875, was back during the early 1880s in a modified form.[15] Other styles saw similar comings and goings.

Women's clothing, together with men's, was still made entirely of natural fibers: silk, wool, cotton, or linen,[16] silk being worn for formal occasions, linen and cotton for informal summer wear, and wool for winter.

Although all garments were completely hand-sewn during the first half of the century, by the 1870s the clothes of middle-class women were principally sewn by machine. Ordinarily, the young woman herself sewed her own clothes even before she was married, although the more intricate and expensive dresses, earlier and later, were made by skilled dressmakers.[17]

In the nineteenth century, women's dresses were enormously complicated, dressmakers having over four hundred different fabrics from which to choose.[18] As an example, the following is a description of a "simple" travelling dress in 1881:

a skirt of blue-grey summer cashmere with twelve pleated flounces of the same material, edged with white Breton lace. Bodice of plaid cashmere, in two shades of blue-gray, fastened down in front with buttons, and draped below the waist in horizontal folds, which fall *en echarpe* at the back. Turned-down collar of plain grey-blue cashmere, with bow of grosgrain ribbon. Tight sleeves of plaid cashmere, with cuffs of plain material. Waistband of grey-blue corded silk.[19]

The dress of course was long, reaching to the floor.

Still, styles and vagaries of accepted fashion in women's clothing (dresses, undergarments, outer garments, and costume accessories such as parasols, muffs, and so forth) and, to a lesser extent, those of her children and husband, appreciably affected how the middle-class married woman spent her day and distributed her husband's surplus income. All these clothes had to be sewn, they had to be washed and cleaned, and they had to be bought as ready-to-wear garments once such advances appeared in the shops. For that reason, knowing about the clothing that was worn in the last quarter of the century gives an insight to many of the woman's priorities.

In 1875 a woman's day dress, that is, the one she wore outside the home when visiting or shopping, was comparatively simple. It consisted of a long bodice that fitted the figure and rose at least to the base of the neck, with long sleeves and a small waist, worn over a skirt of the same material that came down to the shoes; it had no train or bustle.[20] One style in that decade that lasted for two or three years was particularly adaptable for everyday wear in the home (and possibly was the basic dress modified and worn when cleaning the house): the "handkerchief" dress, whose tunic over a narrow kilted or pleated skirt was made in squares, of all materials but especially washable ones.[21]

But simplicity came and went. The bustle, as previously mentioned, common in the early 1870s and then dropped, returned in the 1880s with looped steels inserted in the lining of the skirt to give the proper "bulge" to the back of the skirt.[22] Later in the decade, heavy vertical pleating of wool and serge became part of the skirt, with velveteen and sateen as favorite textiles for the daytime,[23] in a movement away from simplicity toward something more voluminous with much more flouncing than before.[24]

Evening dresses up to 1885 were the same as fashionable day dresses, differing only in the amount of décolletage and fabric, although much more richly ornamented, often with elaborate bead embroidery.[25] Ball dresses by the mid-1880s had a deep V-shaped line or heart-shaped curve in front,[26] with short sleeves; it was worn with long buttoned gloves.

One popular and simple sheath-like form for both day and evening dresses in the 1870s led to a special type of dress in the late 1870s and early 1880s that survived into succeeding decades: the tea gown. With its loose, unboned bodice, a princess form, and a "Watteau" back, falling as a wide box pleat from the shoulder,[27] it offered a comfortable home alternative to the day dress and was the most relaxed and easiest to wear of any style of dress.[28]

Victorian women wore many forms of undergarments, some quite elaborate. Underlinens as chemises and petticoats were worn next to the skin to protect the clothing from body dirt, and structural underwear such as corsets converted the natural body shape into whatever shape was then fashionable. The corset was made of strips of whalebone or steel sandwiched in between layers of fabric,[29] and its length and form varied as the shapes of skirts, the rise and width of the waistline, and the elaborateness of the petticoats changed through the years.[30] At the beginning, linen was the usual material, but by 1875 corsets were made of silk and had grown quite elegant, being in color with trimmings of lace and ribbon.[31] As a basic undergarment, the corset remained as part of the female wardrobe well into the twentieth century.

Another undergarment, considerably less elegant, came into use with the popular sheath dresses in the late 1870s, combining the chemise and the drawers into one piece. It was called, appropriately, "the combination,"[32] and was described as "of particularly aggressive plainness."[33]

For outdoor wear, mantles, with fitted backs but loose in front, were common garments. These differed from coats in that the sleeves fell as capes from the shoulders; they also were usually longer so only the hem of the dress could be seen, although short mantles were also to be found.[34]

Every costume had its accessories, all part of the fashion statement and extremely important. By 1875, young matrons no longer wore caps indoors (a symbol of servility required earlier in the century),[35] but out-of-doors headwear was essential. The most popular material for hats was stiffened plaited straw,[36] and a very popular style in the late 1870s was the "post-boy" hat, its crown shaped like an upturned flowerpot, with a narrow brim.[37] Gloves, required for out-of-doors wear, were also worn indoor with evening dresses, sometimes reaching well above the elbow, sometimes of twenty-button length.[38]

Women's shoes took on heels in the 1860s; by 1875, the heels had become tapered, rising to one-and-one-half or two inches in height; at the same time the toes of the shoe became more and more pointed and remained so throughout the 1880s.[39]

Nor was that the end of fashion as far as women were concerned. Styles in accessories such as parasols and umbrellas, handbags and purses, fans, shawls, furs, and feathers, in various shapes and colors, all had their specialized uses with fashions that waxed and waned, year by year.[40]

Still, one must put these modes of fashion into perspective. There was an appreciable difference between what fashion prescriptively insisted must be worn by the fashionable set and what clothing young, middle-class women actually wore. Since cost was always a major factor even before the young woman married, it appears likely that she looked for clothes that were generally in style but not so extreme that they could not be altered, year after year, and still be more or less appropriate. Women of taste could always find a style that suited them, one that was still in fashion.[41]

In addition, there must have been an appreciable difference between the elaborate dresses worn in public for special occasions as made by a dressmaker, and the clothes women wore indoors while doing chores or even heavy housework. In all probability, the latter required a bit of individualized sewing-machine improvising, although no picture or description can be found of the working dress that a young housewife actually wore while doing (not just supervising) window washing or floor scrubbing in the home.

However, one must not presume that young middle-class women resisted the dictates of fashion just because the dresses were too expensive, or that the young girl had any reservations about their beauty and stylishness. She agreed completely with Mrs. Beeton that, no matter how absurd the prevailing fashion may appear, it never looked as ridiculous as one that was conspicuously out of style, no matter how convenient or comfortable that one may be.[42] For this reason dress-reform movements did not appeal to the middle-class matron. Many more years of living had to follow before she began to doubt the dictates of prevailing fashion and recognize that, in many cases, the styles were inappropriate or over-elaborate for the occasion. Her solution in the early years was to make private alterations to the dress designs in order to meet her special needs; money (or lack thereof) and her working life at home demanded it.

Moreover, even in public, the dresses a middle-class matron of moderate means wore differed considerably (as is often the case today) from the high fashion insisted upon by Society; high fashion never typified the middle-class lifestyle.[43] Many of the vociferous discussions by medical experts in women's magazines about the dangers of contracting consumption by wearing low-cut dresses or thin shoes or the evil health effects of excessively tight corset lacing were irrelevant to her (except as topics of conversation, perhaps).[44] Despite the durable fashion insistence on the allure of the tiny waist, Dr. Alice Kerr, who lectured regularly on female health, put it succinctly: "I am not going to say anything about tight stays because I never yet met anyone who wore them tight."[45] Women who lived and worked in the home were not given to parading around in thin shoes or to tying their stays so tightly as to affect their health or their movements.

In reality, the looks and the fashions of the young woman's wardrobe when she married were drawn from her pre-marital life as learned from her mother before her. How this would inevitably change as she went about in public would depend on a number of variables, such as income, friends, the priority of household duties, pressure to conform to outside opinion and—in the end—her own good sense.

NOTES

1. L.C.B. Seaman, *Victorian England: Aspects of English and Imperial History, 1837–1901* (London: Methuen, 1973), 440.
2. Branca, *Silent Sisterhood*, 62.
3. Ibid., 70; also Mitchell, *Daily Life*, 193.
4. Cynthia L. White, *Women's Magazines, 1693–1968* (London: Michael Joseph, 1970), 75. A list appears on 310–11.
5. Bott and Clephane, *Our Mothers*, 190.
6. *Ward & Lock's Home Book: A Domestic Encyclopedia* (London: Ward, Lock & Co., n.d.), 527–63.
7. Ibid., 565–82.
8. Ibid., 565–70.
9. Ibid.
10. Branca, *Silent Sisterhood*, 127.
11. Ibid.
12. Roger Hart, *English Life in the Nineteenth Century* (New York: G. P. Putnam's Sons, 1971), 105.
13. E. S. Turner, *What the Butler Saw: Two Hundred and Fifty Years of the Servant Problem* (New York: St. Martin's Press, 1963), 132.
14. Bott and Clephane, *Our Mothers*, 197.
15. Christina Walkley and Varda Foster, *Crinolines and Crimping Irons: Victorian Clothes, How They Were Cleaned and Cared For* (London: Peter Owen, 1978), 26.
16. Ibid., 15.
17. Ibid., also Mitchell, *Daily Life*, 138.
18. Mitchell, *Victorian Britain*, 175.
19. Gloag, *Victorian Comfort*, 167, the illustration caption from an article in *Sylvia's Home Journal* (1881).
20. Anne Buck, *Victorian Costumes and Costume Accessories* (New York: Thomas Nelson & Sons, 1961), 59.
21. Ibid., 61.
22. Ibid., 62.
23. Walkley and Foster, *Crinolines and Crimping Irons*, 27.
24. Buck, *Victorian Costume*, 61.
25. Ibid., 64.
26. Ibid.

27. Ibid., 66.
28. Ibid.
29. Walkley and Foster, *Crinolines and Crimping Irons*, 40.
30. Ibid., 41.
31. Buck, *Victorian Costume*, 87.
32. Ibid., 91.
33. Bott and Clephane, *Our Mothers*, 199.
34. Buck, *Victorian Costume*, 102.
35. Walkley and Foster, *Crinolines and Crimping Irons*, 71.
36. Ibid., 74–75.
37. Ibid., 79.
38. Ibid., 87.
39. Buck, *Victorian Costume*, 151, 159.
40. Walkley and Foster, *Crinolines and Crimping Irons*, 114–18, 140–46, ff.
41. R.C.K. Ensor, *England, 1870–1914* (Oxford: Clarendon Press, 1988), 168.
42. Beeton, *Book of Household Management*, 12.
43. Branca, *Silent Sisterhood*, 10.
44. Ibid., 66.
45. As quoted in Branca, *Silent Sisterhood*, 66.

PART II

THE REALITY: LIFE IN GREATER LONDON, 1875–1900

CHAPTER 5

The Housewife as Lowly Domestic: Cleaning the House and Doing the Laundry

For the first time in her life, the young middle-class woman now found herself in a position of authority. As mistress of the house, she was "in charge," although she was not yet aware of what her duties were or of their complexity.

Still, those jobs that had to do with keeping house were familiar ones. Cleaning the house, washing dishes and pots in the kitchen, and doing the laundry were activities with which she felt comfortable because she probably had done them before when single and living at home with her parents.[1] Now in her own many-roomed house, she knew she would have to do them again. For the housecleaning, she would need to hire a live-in maid-of-all-work (as her mother may also have done) but, given the amount of work and the size of the house, she knew she would have to do some physical work as well.

There was a great deal involved in cleaning the Victorian house, although the new bride quickly learned that trying to do all the cleaning tasks detailed in the various domestic manuals was quite unrealistic.[2] Still, even when pared down to what could be accomplished, the number of chores to be done by herself and her house maid was formidable.

A brief daily schedule of daily housecleaning tasks in 1875, even at a minimum level, was something like the following.[3]

Before breakfast the fire in the kitchen coal stove, winter and summer, had be rekindled and water put up to heat. Upstairs (up one flight of stairs), the shutters and the drapes in the public rooms (i.e., the dining room, sitting room or parlor, study or drawing room) were opened, the grates cleaned and a new fire laid in each fireplace (in all seasons but summer), and the entry hall and the front steps swept. All downstairs lamps were taken to the basement to be cleaned, their wicks trimmed and returned to the ground floor.

Then, upstairs (up two flights of stairs) the fire in the master bedroom had to be lit in winter and hot water brought up from the kitchen. (In homes with many servants, the housemaids brought up many ewers of water for baths for the master and mistress before breakfast, but this doesn't seem possible in one-servant homes, given the limited time and womanpower available.) Then it was back to the kitchen (down three flights of stairs) where breakfast preparation was underway.

If a hired cook were on duty, the mistress would not be in the kitchen but up in her bedroom washing up and dressing at a leisurely pace. But if there was no hired cook, the housewife was already up, bathed or washed and dressed by the time the maid brought up hot water to the master, working in the kitchen preparing the family breakfast. When breakfast was ready, it was brought up to the dining room by the servant (up one flight of stairs) and placed on the sideboard for her husband and herself (and, later, the children) to eat.

The housemaid had her breakfast in the kitchen at the same time (one flight down). After the master left for work in the city, the food and dishes were removed, the dishes washed, and the kitchen cleaned. Then the major housework of the day began.

The servant began with the bedrooms (three flights up from the basement): beds aired and made, the floors mopped and all surfaces dusted. The wash basins and chamber pots then were carried down to the basement (where the drain pipes were), emptied and cleaned, and the clean basins and pots returned to the rooms (three flights up).

Then the housemaid went downstairs (first down to the ground floor, then up one flight to the first floor) to clean the public rooms: every object in each room dusted, the floors mopped or hand-scrubbed, the carpets swept or hand-spotted to rid them of the dirt tracked in from the streets the day before.

(Although a mechanical carpet sweeper was invented by Melville Bissell in 1876,[4] it was not on the British market until 1880. The invention most needed to make the cleaning of the rugs and drapes easier did not appear until after the turn of the century at some point after 1901, when Mr. Cecil Booth invented the electric-driven vacuum cleaner.)[5]

While this was going on, the housewife was in the kitchen, dealing with the dairyman, greengrocer, and butcher who came by regularly to see what food she (or the cook) wanted to order for dinner. If the providers did not ordinarily stop by, the housewife went out to do the day's marketing; because there was no household refrigeration, perishables had to be bought every day.[6]

Luncheon was prepared by the cook or the housewife-as-cook and served in the dining room. In later years, if there were children, the children would join their mother for lunch. After the mistress ate her lunch and the food and dishes were removed and washed, the house maid sat down to eat lunch.

The domestic help spent the afternoon finishing up whatever cleaning chores had not been completed in the morning. In the kitchen, the housewife (or cook) made early preparations for dinner. If there was any free time before tea, she usually spent it mending clothes or linens, darning stockings, or doing sewing jobs on her sewing machine.

If the family had tea between four and five P.M., this third meal of the day was served but not in the dining room; tea was taken in the drawing room in what someone described as an indoor-picnic setting.[7] Tea was prepared in an urn that was brought up (two flights from the basement), together with the plates, flatware, and assorted tasties to eat, later to be carried down again, two flights, to the kitchen. After tea, the dishes and pots in the kitchen were washed.

The table was then set for dinner by the servant while the housewife (or cook) prepared dinner. (The cooking and the service of the dinner—no small thing—will be discussed later.)

Once dinner was eaten, the dishes were cleared off the table and sideboard and carried off to the basement (down one flight). The servant then had a light supper by herself in the kitchen before washing up the dishes, scouring and putting away the pots and pans, cleaning the stove, stoking the fire in the stove and damping it down, and getting the kitchen ready for the next morning.

Then all the bedrooms were revisited (up two and three flights of stairs), to turn down the bed covers, lay out the night clothes, remove the dirty chamber pots and the wash basins for cleaning, then returning them to the bedrooms. The servant also laid the fires (if it was customary in this house to have a bedroom fire) for the next morning.

On Saturday, of course, ordinary jobs had to be done with particular diligence in preparation for the Sunday sabbath.[8]

In addition to the routine jobs done daily, there were special tasks that had to be done at periodic intervals: cleaning the wallpaper, polishing the silver plate and the "brights" around the house, brushing down the drapes, washing the windows inside and out (the last at less frequent intervals), and washing down the springs of beds with a corrosive solution to discourage bugs.[9]

Then there were the seasonal tasks, the most formidable being spring cleaning. In spring, the winter drapes were taken down and replaced by summer ones, winter clothes laid away and lighter garments brought out, the chimneys were swept, the carpets taken up and beaten clean, rooms were newly papered where needed, and everything was washed and freshened up in anticipation of warm weather. If she could afford it, the housewife sometimes hired temporary outside help.[10]

In summer and into the fall, food preparation for the winter was done; fruits and vegetables were purchased in quantity and prepared as jams and sweet preserves, pickles and ketchups, and condiments of many kinds.[11]

At the end of autumn, the reverse of spring cleaning took place: summer clothes were exchanged for winter clothing and summer curtains taken down and replaced by winter drapes. Most important of all, repairs to the structure of the house were undertaken then by outside contractors to make sure that everything be in good working condition before winter's onset, and the work of these operators possibly was supervised by the housewife.

Except for Christmas preparations, nothing special was planned for the winter, the ordinary winter tasks making enough extra work for the servant. The most strenuous of these were tasks associated with heating the house: ashes from the fireplaces had to be removed and carried down to the basement where they were placed in disposal bins for pick-up by the dustman, kindling and coal had to be carried up to the rooms, the grates cleaned and polished or blackened, and new fires laid. Often this had to be done two and three times a day.

Housecleaning was difficult enough based on the number of rooms alone, but other factors compounded the problem. One of them, of which the housewife herself may not have been aware, was the awkward shape of her house and inconvenient arrangement of rooms. Because the typical Victorian home was built with many rooms stacked up on successive floors, the housewife and her servant were continually climbing steep risers up constricted stairwells simply to get from one room to another.

Poor lighting was a major problem considering the work

that had to be done. If the house was part of a terrace, natural light came in only through windows facing the front and the back. Even if the newlyweds were able to rent a semi-attached home, one step up on the economic scale from the terraced home, the separation from the house on the unattached wall side was only a few feet, hardly enough to admit much light.

Artificial lighting was no better, at least initially. In 1875, light was provided by oil or kerosene lamps[12] whose wicks had to be constantly trimmed and soot-covered glass chimneys regularly cleaned. Early gas-jet lighting, an open flame burning in a wall bracket, produced little illumination.[13] Even though this was improved when a device called the Welsbach incandescent gas mantle was added in the mid-1880s, gas lighting was still not available on the upper floors that had to be cleaned.

In 1875, piped water entered the house only in the basement; this meant that whoever was doing the cleaning had to continuously climb the stairs to empty dirty water or to get clean water for the scrub pails.

The form and abundance of furniture and furnishings made normal housework harder than it might otherwise have been. As previously mentioned, the furniture was heavy and ornate—and there was a great deal of it, with many freestanding objects occupying whatever floor space was not covered by pieces of furniture, with photographs, mementos, and diaries on every horizontal surface above the floor. The dusting required more than just a casual flick of the feather duster; each small object on each table, shelf, or mantel had to be lifted separately, carefully dusted, and replaced before going to the next one. Compared to the public rooms, the bedrooms were sparsely furnished, but even these were overcrowded so that cleaning had to be done carefully to make sure nothing was knocked over. In all, the house was a difficult environment to keep clean.

Then there was the laundry and dry-cleaning of clothes. In general, women's day dresses and men's suits were not washable, so they were not part of the laundry; but even excluding these, the laundry was huge, although the family was small. It included, as a minimum, the man's shirts, his underwear, the housewife's underwear and petticoats (in large number), dresses worn by the housewife and the servant while cleaning house (which, by design, were washable), undergarments of the servant, everyone's night clothing, table linen and kitchen towels, servants' aprons and caps, collars and cuffs, bath towels, and bed linen.[14] In later years children's washables also were included.

Whatever was in any way washable had to be washed, then starched and ironed by hand.

In wealthier homes the washing was sent out to laundresses, but in the household of this income bracket, washday ordinarily was an in-house task.[15] It was not ordinarily a weekly occurance since doing it totally disrupted the daily routine. Usually, "washday" was spread over several days,[16] involving the full attention of the general servant and the housewife. Sometimes, if overwhelmed, the housewife hired a temporary washerwoman to come in to help with the work.[17]

The process began the night before with clothes being soaked in large vats of water overnight. On washday, extra water was boiled in huge quantities on the kitchen stove, then the water carried to the tubs in the basement into which the wash, taken out of the soak water and wrung out, was placed. Here the clothes were scrubbed on corrugated zinc or iron scrubbing boards.[18]

There were a variety of soaps, whiteners, bleaches, fixatives (for colored items), and starches used for the laundry in 1875, some general-purpose, others specialized for particular materials; all were rather complicated to use but easy enough to purchase.[19] (Unfortunately, many of these products were harsh on the skin, as both the servant and housewife knew, but since no one used rubber gloves, the ill effects of the cleaning products on their hands could not be avoided.)

Sometimes a "washing dolly," a post with "arms" and

"legs," was used to beat the clothes in soapy water to get the dirt out[20] but, as yet, no efficient, labor-saving washing machine was on the market. One washer, a wooden tub with a rough interior that was filled with clothes, water, and soap and then rocked or rotated to circulate the clothing, was available but the machine was both hard on the fabrics and, being hand-operated, as tiring to use as a scrubbing board.[21] Another device called "The Torpedo," a cigar-shaped tub operated by steam, came on the market in the 1890s but was dangerous to operate; it could not have been in widespread use in many homes.[22] (Not until 1911, when a man in Newton, Iowa, called Frederick Maytag patented an electrically driven washing machine and wringer[23] did the housewife get the revolutionary device she so desperately needed to effectively wash the family clothing.)

After the clothes were rinsed in many baths of rinse water, the separate pieces were sent through a hand-turned wringer and hung up to dry. If there was no access to an outside area for drying, the clothes had to be dried inside, sometimes on clothes-horses or airers, often on enormous drying racks that were hoisted up to the ceiling out of the way.[24]

After the clothes dried, they were examined for tears, with torn pieces put aside for later mending. Then the petticoats, shirts, bed linen, table linen, cuffs and collars, servants' caps and aprons, and other such items were starched and finally ironed. Flatwear (bed linen, table linen, towels, and so forth) were not hand-ironed but smoothed out by feeding them through a large wringer mechanism called a mangle.[25] All other clothes were ironed on a board with a flat metal iron heated on the range or a box iron into which hot coals could be placed. (An early electric iron, invented in 1882, was very dangerous to use; not until 1904 did models appear that were safe enough to be used on a regular basis.)[26]

Finally, the clothing was returned to the drawers, cupboards or trunks where they were ordinarily kept. They were not hung up on hangers, however; no mention is made of the device we know as the clothes hanger until late in the 1890s.[27] Clothes that could not be laid flat in drawers or on long shelves were hung up on pegs or laid over rods. Sometimes they were "unpicked," that is, their stitching was taken out so they could lay flat (which meant that, before they could be worn, they had to be sewn back together again).[28]

Articles of clothing that could not be washed were carefully checked for spots and the soiled portions cleaned separately by a variety of cleaning fluids. Although commercial dry-cleaning compounds were unknown in the 1870s (except to clean specialized items such as fur or lace),[29] a number of common household compounds were traditionally used to do the job,[30] and new products in ready-to-use packages gradually appeared on the market to make the clothes cleaning easier.

It is unlikely that the housewife did much else besides the laundry on the day set aside as washday. But how much of the other housework she had to do, including preparation of food for the family on washing days, depended on how reliable her maid-of-all-work was and whether or not she could afford a cook. As part of her job, she allocated the jobs to be done between herself and the servant, probably reserving for herself the lighter jobs, if that was possible, and doing whatever tasks required managerial or administrative skills. Even then, the sheer physical labor involved in the daily housecleaning and doing the laundry, making no allowances for all the other jobs she also had to do, was enormous. There must have been days when the housewife as domestic dragged herself to bed at night, as totally exhausted as her maid-of-all-work, wondering whether it was all worthwhile.

NOTES

1. Branca, *Silent Sisterhood*, 47.
2. Erna Olafson Hellerstein, Leslie Parker Hume, and Karen M. Offen, eds. *Victorian Women: A Documentary Account of Women's*

Lives in Nineteenth Century England, France, and the United States (Stanford, Calif.: Stanford University Press, 1981), 278–79.

3. The enumeration of daily and seasonal household duties has been constructed from lists that appeared in Mrs. Beeton's *Book of Household Managment, Spons' Household Manual: A Treasury of Domestic Receipts and Guide for Home Management* (London: E. & F. N. Spons, 1887); and Jane Panton, *From Kitchen to Garret: Hints for Young Householders* (London: Ward & Downey, 1890). Information on the duties of the domestic servants was taken from Pamala Horn, *The Rise and Fall of the Victorian Servant* (Dublin: Gill & Macmillan, 1975); E. S. Turner, *What the Butler Saw*; and Frank E. Huggett, *Life Below Stairs: Domestic Servants in England from Victorian Times* (London: John Murray, 1977), modified as necessary to fit a household of this size and character.

4. Wilson, *Life in a Victorian House*, 21.

5. Davidson, *A Woman's Work*, 129.

6. "The first household refrigerator patent was issued to Albert T. Marshall in 1899, but the first domestic-use refrigerator was not manufactured until 1913." From Nell DuVall, *Domestic Technology: A Chronology of Developments* (Boston: G. K. Hall, 1988), 57.

7. Mitchell, *Daily Life*, 127.

8. Turner, *What the Butler Saw*, 150.

9. Ibid., 149.

10. Beeton, *Book of Household Management*, 35–36.

11. Ibid., 36.

12. Davidson, *A Woman's Work*, 109. The kerosene lamps, developed in the United States, were sold in Britain on a large scale after the 1860s as an inexpensive light source. In England, kerosene is known as paraffin.

13. Mitchell, *Victorian Britain*, 452–53.

14. Walkley and Foster, *Crinolines and Crimping Irons*, 50.

15. Ibid., 54.

16. Ibid., 64.

17. Ibid., 51.

18. Ibid., 50–60.

19. Ibid., 58–63, where the authors explain them in great detail. A list appears in the book's appendix, 180–83, of seventy-two different Victorian cleaning agents.

20. Wilson, *Life in a Victorian House*, 30.

21. Walkley and Foster, *Crinolines and Crimping Irons*, 51.
22. Ibid., 51–52.
23. DuVall, *Domestic Technology*, 200.
24. Walkley and Foster, *Crinolines and Crimping Irons*, 63.
25. Ibid., 58.
26. Wilson, *Life in a Victorian House*, 31.
27. Walkley and Foster, *Crinolines and Crimping Irons*, 168.
28. Ibid., 13.
29. Ibid., 29.
30. Ibid., 32–38. For example, rubbing a cut raw potato on black clothes removed dirt, a weak solution of carbonate of soda cleaned French merino (a fine wool and silk cloth), stale bread removed surface grease spots, and turpentine cleaned velvet. Gin, which was plentiful and cheap then, was used as a cleaning fluid and so was diluted liquid ammonia. Many other products for cleaning natural fibers are listed here.

CHAPTER 6

The Housewife as Specialized Domestic: Preparing the Meals and Clothing the Family

Housecleaning was often drudgery, but other household jobs were more fulfilling. Cooking together with marketing and the management of the family's clothes involved skills the housewife already had to some degree, and their exercise called for decision-making talents she either had or could easily learn. The work certainly was far more challenging than doing menial housecleaning chores.

If our young married woman had shown any interest in cooking and baking when she was younger, then this part of housewifery was easily taken care. She now happily became the cook, and part of her enjoyment lay in the satisfaction of saving up to £60 a year by eliminating the need to hire a cook. However, even if she had no interest in cooking, the housewife often became the cook simply because they could not afford to hire one.

Besides preparing meals, the job included menu planning, marketing, and preserving food for future consumption, tasks which the advice manuals assured her were her responsibility whether she did the cooking or not. In addition, she was expected to learn the cost of foodstuffs in order to choose between competing vendors and also to properly budget food expenditures as part of the cost of running the household.[1] Inevitably, the job also (unhappily) included such kitchen chores as washing the cooking pots and pans, cleaning and blackening the stove, scrubbing the sinks and tables, mopping the floors, and cleaning the passages and kitchen stairs[2]—unless she, the housewife-as-cook, could divert her general servant from the housecleaning to take over as kitchen scullion.

As mentioned previously, the cook's domain, the basement kitchen, was not a particularly congenial workplace. The natural lighting was poor, coming in through windows facing below-street-level areaways both in the front and back. Unless the house had venting inlets and outlets to permit smells to exit,[3] these windows had to be kept open so that through-ventilation could dissipate the cooking odors.

The dominating piece of equipment in the kitchen at that time was the cast-iron coal-burning close range, with a fire chamber surrounding the oven box in the center and a moveable iron plate on top for cooking in pots and pans.[4] (At some later date, the range would be equipped with an attached boiler for heating water, but in 1875, such a hot-water boiler probably was not in place.)

A fire in the range, then, had to be fed continuously, both for cooking and to heat water for washing and cleaning, making the kitchen unbearably hot in the summer. (Later in the century, when a gas range could be purchased to replace the coal-burning stove, its major attraction was that "the comparative coolness make cooking a pleasure to many who cannot stand for any length of time near a coal range.")[5]

To relieve the heat, eliminate cooking odors, and dispel smells from the drain pipes that converged in the kitchen before exiting to outside sewer pipes, a really efficient ventilation system was needed. But it is doubtful if such a system was installed in a home built before 1875 for rental purposes; whatever venting the builder provided probably was minimal.

The business of being the cook began, of course, with "the

art of cookery," as the English called it, a learned method of preparing food that was peculiarly English. If the housewife was not already a passable cook and had no relatives nearby to help her, she learned to cook by following the recipes found in the many domestic manuals and women's magazines available at the time. Mrs. Beeton's *Book of Household Management* was primarily a cookbook, with over one thousand pages devoted to recipes of all sorts of dishes, including some very exotic and elaborate French recipes and menus.[6] However, Mrs. Beeton also printed menus of "good plain dinners" for every month of the year, and these proved to be the staples of family cuisine.[7] In the 1880s, many new magazines directed to the inexperienced housewife contained advice on cooking skills, recipes, and instruction on various housekeeping duties.[8]

All the domestic manuals printed an enormous amount of advice about marketing for food. *Spons' Household Manual*, for example, devoted almost twenty single-spaced pages, in six-point type, to advise on how to shop for the best meat, fish, game, poultry, fruits and vegetables, broken down by season.[9] Although time-consuming, doing the marketing was work the housewife probably enjoyed since it allowed her to get out of the house and meet tradespeople in their shops. At the beginning, of course, she was not very expert at recognizing good quality or reasonable prices, but this skill came in time. It was a job she was urged to undertake whether experienced or not; the advice manuals regularly cautioned her not to delegate marketing to a servant. Domestics who dealt with the tradesmen, she was warned, were often tempted by vendors who promised to give the servant a "commission" for the family's exclusive custom, the cost of which eventually turned up in higher food bills.[10]

Without refrigeration, food shopping for perishables was done daily. (By the end of the century, an ice-chest or "ice-safe" was occasionally installed in the larder but only for such extremely perishable products as milk and possibly butter.)[11]

However, the housewife was not always required to go to the store in person, since the dairyman, butcher, fishmonger, and greengrocer often took the initiative, when the family moved in, of visiting the housewife to solicit her patronage.[12] Once the specific vendors were chosen, they came by each morning, either with the standing order or to find out, and later deliver, what was needed on that particular day.

The grocer provided the housewife with nonperishables such as tea, cocoa, coffee, oatmeal, crackers, vinegar, molasses, currants and raisins, flour, spices, sugar, honey, macaroni, and rice.[13] He also stocked such household staples as soap, candles, starch, matches, firewood, brushes, baskets and brooms, petroleum, and lamps.[14] All food items were sold in bulk, the shopkeeper measuring out the required amount from storage bins and wrapping the product in paper for the woman to carry home.

On occasion, the housewife purchased grocery items in bulk in order to save money, ordering them by post from stores outside of the neighborhood; the goods would then be shipped to her home.[15] However, this required a large initial outlay of cash, which she did not often have.

Since nothing was known about vitamins until the early twentieth century or of the negative effects of too much sugar or fats, the cook had few guidelines for knowing which foods were the best for the health of her family. One textbook on domestic economy divided all food into three categories, nitrogenous, carbonaceous, and inorganic, and explained how much to eat of each.[16] Mrs. Beeton printed a "digestive time table," showing how long it took for certain foods to be digested, since she recommended that only foods that could be digested in four to four-and-one-half hours (with some exceptions) were to be part of the family diet.[17] To judge from the model menus printed by Mrs. Beeton, meals were regularly short of fresh vegetables; when vegetables were cooked, the recommended cooking time was from twenty minutes to one and a half hours.[18] However, because a varied diet was recommended, including seasonal fruits and vegetables, a healthful diet may sometimes have been inadvertently achieved.

Next to choosing food that she was able to cook and that was pleasing to her husband, the housewife was most interested in the cost of the food, since food accounted for almost 50 percent of the family's expenditures.[19] Precisely how the household money was distributed for food and household goods will be discussed later as part of the total family finances.

Another essential part of food preparation was planning the menus and determining how and when the food was to be served. If the housewife had had no experience in this area, she again would find all the help she needed, and more, in the domestic manuals and women's magazines devoted to the subject.

The method of serving meals in the Victorian home involved a very convoluted eating etiquette: what food to prepare for whom, when the meals were to be served, and where, and how, and who ate or did not eat with whom were all closely regulated matters—and not only in the homes of the wealthy. There were the ordinary meals for the man and wife, special meals served for guests, meals to be served separately for the help and not necessarily from the same menu, meals prepared for the children that were not only different from those eaten by the adults but also served separately, and at a different time, and not ordinarily eaten in the company of their parents. Dinner, in particular, constituted a complicated social ritual which was described in great and elaborate detail in Mrs. Beeton's *Book of Household Management*.[20]

However, despite the meticulous attention given by the domestic manuals to fine food preparation, it is unlikely that the cooks hired in most middle-class homes were skilled enough to prepare the elaborate cuisine suggested.[21] There were no training schools for cooks at all until 1860, when a Mrs. Mitchell opened a cookery school in London to teach "professed" cookery to servants[22]; and even when more schools opened in London in the 1880s, it is doubtful whether their influence was enough to make much difference in standards of cooking.[23]

It is also doubtful whether the complicated eating protocol of the upper classes was followed in the households of the moderate-income middle-class, considering the money restraints and limited household help. It is more likely that the middle-class meal routine would be close to the following:

Breakfast was the first food eaten for the day; it is unlikely that anyone was available to make, much less deliver, tea and a sweet biscuit to the master as he was dressing, as was done in wealthier homes. The housewife prepared breakfast and saw that it was served up in the dining room any time between 7:30 and 9 A.M., depending on the master's work schedule. The same type of breakfast eaten by the adult householders was also given to the servants and, later, the children. (The incidence of servants being fed skimpy, unpalatable diets was more characteristic of early Victorian years than of the 1870s, if for no other reason than that servants were harder to retain and good food was one means of keeping them happy.)

This meal was substantial and generally hot. Possible foods were broiled herring, baked or grilled mackerel, meat turnovers or patties, cold or home-potted meat, broiled bacon, poached, boiled, or fried eggs, fried potato chips, and porridge—plus toast with marmalade, English muffins, tea, coffee, or cocoa.[24]

Luncheon was a light meal prepared by the housewife and eaten at 1 or 2 P.M.; later, when there were children, they ate with her. The servant, who ate in the kitchen, usually ate the same food as the family. A luncheon menu might consist of cabbage, potatoes, onions, meat and fish, with bread and possibly inexpensive fruit.[25] (Mrs. Beeton suggested that an ordinary luncheon, while having fewer courses than dinner as a rule, have almost identical food, although she did give a simplified menu that eliminated the hors d'oeuvre, suggested either soup or fish, and advised a comparatively simple sweet course.)[26]

Tea was not a meal so much as a light refreshment break to be served between luncheon and dinner. Laid out in the drawing room (not the dining room) between four and five in the afternoon, the housewife ate alone (or in later years with the children, this being their evening meal). If she had no guests, she served herself. If there were guests, however, the maid was present (in "company" clothes) to pass around cups of tea and the thin bread-and-butter sandwiches, cake, or sometimes, fresh fruit.[27]

For the adults in the family, the big meal was dinner, served at about 8 P.M.,[28] which the housewife-as-cook spent all afternoon preparing. Even if there were no guests, the meal was fairly formal, the husband and wife eating alone. (The children, if any, were either in bed or preparing for bed.)[29]

The social ritual governing dinner in the Victorian home regulated the number of courses served and the fastidious preparation, placement, and serving of each course (which included soup, fish, sauces and gravies, vegetables, entrees, pastries, and various condiments), as well as detailed settings and meticulous service, even when the family was not entertaining guests.[30]

It seems unlikely that such an elaborate format was regularly followed in less-wealthy households, if only because it is hard to envision the simple maid-of-all-work positioning the polished silver and centerpiece on the table; preparing the meticulously detailed place settings; serving the dishes *á la française* (with the food laid out and kept warm on the sideboard, then served one course at a time); or *á la russe* (carving the food on the sideboard; placing it onto platters and then circling the table constantly; and offering it to guests in no particular course order.)[31] Nor is it likely that the housewife could routinely concoct the eight-course menu (soup, fish, entrees, remove, roast, sweets, savoury, and dessert) that Mrs.

Beeton suggested (printed in her book, with diagrams) as a model of the respectable dinner to be served.[32]

A more normal dinner meal for husband and wife (and the servant in the kitchen), at least during the couple's early married life, probably consisted of what Mrs. Beeton called "plain family dinners": two or three courses of simply prepared foods served "English style," that is, with the food placed on the table and ladled out, carved, or served from there.

Providing for and supervising the clothing needs of the family (other than doing the laundry and dry cleaning) was the other major job done by the housewife as "specialized domestic." It required making or purchasing clothing for herself and later for the children, and sewing whatever garments her husband needed which were not purchased directly from his tailor and haberdasher. Her husband's clothing was not her responsibility; he dealt directly with these retailers, ordering his made-to-order suits, coats, and headwear on his own. Later, he would purchase his ready-to-wear garments from them as well.

The advent of the sewing machine, the first major domestic labor-saving device in the Victorian home, was of critical importance to the housewife. Invented in 1845 by the American Elias Howe and widely marketed throughout the world by Isaac Singer,[33] the sewing machine first was adopted for industrial use—but the consumer was also to profit from this industrial development because it brought ready-to-wear clothing, boots, and shoes onto the retail market.[34]

In the 1860s a concerted effort was made to market the machine directly to the consumer, and the middle-class housewife immediately saw its possibilities as a labor-saving and money-saving instrument. She not only used it for mending clothing and household linens but, more importantly, began making her own dresses and undergarments, aprons, and dresses as well as shirts and underclothes for her husband.[35] Later she would also make clothes and underwear for the children. Although the machines ranged in price from an inexpensive £6 model made by W. F. Thomas to the best but expensive Singer machine selling for up to £15,[36] she did what she had to to own one, even buying it through hire-purchase (the installment plan) when necessary.[37] The housewife with free time in the afternoon was far more likely to spend it at the family sewing machine than in making social calls. For the first time, it was possible to make a man's shirt in just over an hour where before it would have taken 14½ hours by hand; or to make herself a chemise in less than an hour instead of the 10½ hour hand-sewing job.[38] No wonder the middle-class married woman welcomed the domestic sewing machine with such enthusiasm!

In 1850, the woman's magazine, *The World of Fashion*, began to print dress patterns, distributing them free with the magazine as an advertising ploy, and this means of providing dress patterns for women who made their own clothing proved so popular that other domestic magazines quickly followed suit.[39]

Although the sewing machine was deplored among the monied classes as having a pernicious influence on the fine art of hand-stitching, even Mrs. Isabella Beeton, stalwart traditionalist that she was, applauded the invention without reservation. She wrote: "With the help of this useful invention, a lady can, with perfect comfort, make and mend every article used by herself and children, and do a great deal toward repairing and making her husband's clothes, and this without labour to herself, and at no expense beyond the first outlay."[40] The other household manuals agreed, and many included long and detailed sections on home dressmaking: measurements, patterns, and advice on the cutting and fitting of various pieces of apparel.[41]

However, considering how complicated fashionable dresses for women were, it is probable that most housewives, even those who had to watch their expenditures, did not have the talent for mastering complex dress construction; they would continue to call in a dressmaker for their more elaborate clothing.[42] Still, sewing on a machine, like the art of cooking, was a learned skill that gave the middle-class matron both pleasure and a feeling of professional competence—job satisfaction in a sphere where a sense of inadequacy was too often the norm.

NOTES

1. Beeton, *Book of Household Management*, 11–12; also 32–34, 37–40, chapter 5, "Marketing," and the preliminary observations to the various cookery sections of the book. Instructions detailing the duties of the hired cook and housekeeper applied to the housewife-as-cook as well.
2. Ibid., 38–39, "Duties of the Kitchen-Maid."
3. Ibid., 30, 46.
4. Ibid., 48.
5. Ibid., 53.
6. Ibid. (1880 ed.), chapters 7 through 28.
7. Ibid., 913–52, passim.
8. White, *Women's Magazines*, 75.
9. *Spons' Household Manual*, 563–83.
10. Elizabeth Langland, *Nobody's Angels: Middle-Class Women and Domestic Ideology in Victorian Culture* (Ithaca, N.Y.: Cornell University Press, 1995), 48.
11. Davidson, *A Woman's Work*, 62.
12. Mitchell, *Daily Life*, 131.
13. Ibid.
14. James B. Jefferys, *Retail Trading in Britain, 1850–1950* (Cambridge, U.K.: Cambridge University Press, 1954), 126.
15. Una A. Robertson, *The Illustrated History of the Housewife, 1650–1950* (New York: St. Martin's Press, 1997), 110.
16. W. Jerome Harrison, *The Science of Home Life: A Textbook of Domestic Economy* (London: Thomas Nelson & Sons, 1896), 27–32.
17. Beeton, *Book of Household Management*, 124–25.
18. Ibid., 551–604.

19. John Burnett, *A History of the Cost of Living* (London: Penguin Books, 1969), 239.
20. Beeton, *Book of Household Management*, 1676–1682.
21. Huggett, *Life Below Stairs*, 101.
22. Ibid.
23. Ibid.
24. Wilson, *Life in a Victorian House*, 18; also Beeton, *Book of Household Management* (1880 ed.), 1242.
25. Wilson, *Life in a Victorian House*, 24.
26. Beeton, *Book of Household Management*, 1680.
27. Ibid., 1693.
28. Wilson, *Life in a Victorian House*, 40.
29. Mitchell, *Daily Life*, 148.
30. Beeton, *Book of Household Management*, 1676–82.
31. Robertson, *History of the Housewife*, 34.
32. Beeton, *Book of Household Management*, 1689–90.
33. Alison Adburgham, *Shops and Shopping, 1800–1914: Where and in What Manner the Well-Dressed Englishwoman Bought Her Clothes* (London: Allen & Unwin, 1964), 113–14.
34. Jefferys, *Retail Trading*, 293.
35. Ibid.
36. Branca, *Silent Sisterhood*, 51.
37. Ibid., 52.
38. DuVall, *Domestic Technology*, 164.
39. Adburgham, *Shops and Shopping*, 114–16.
40. Beeton, *Book of Household Management* (1880 ed.), 8.
41. See *Ward & Lock's Home Book*, 779–809.
42. Mitchell, *Daily Life*, 139.

CHAPTER 7

The Housewife as Employer: Managing the Servants

The young married woman knew that managing the servants was expected of her as mistress of her house. Having known servants in her mother's home before she was married, the young bride probably felt that she was perfectly capable of doing what appeared to be a fairly straightforward job: to hire, train, and retain a live-in domestic staff—and to dismiss those who proved unsatisfactory.

However, judging from the letters to the editor that flooded into the offices of women's magazines dealing with domestic matters, the so-called servant problem was a major stress factor for every middle-class and upper-class British matron of the century.[1] With the exception of the art of cookery, it was a subject about which most questions were asked and, in turn, about which advice was most copiously dispensed.[2]

The hiring of a general servant became a priority the moment the woman began housekeeping, given the size of her home and the overwhelming number of chores to be done. Although later she would become involved with hiring and working with servants in other categories, the housewife began learning employer skills in her first encounter with the maid-of-all-work hiring market.

Even though the steady stream of country girls coming into London in search of positions as domestics still had not subsided by 1875 when the housewife was married, it slackened shortly thereafter. Between 1881 and 1901, there was a decrease of over 7 percent in the number of female domestic servants ages 15–20, the pool from which the general maid-of-all-work came.[3] But it was not the decrease in the quantity of girls applying for jobs that the housewife found most disturbing but the lack, in the opinion of the young housewife, of *quality* of domestic help. Given her expectations, it was a problem not easily solved.

The newlywed began her search by asking friends or relatives if they knew of anyone looking for work or, by extension, asking them to ask their servants if they knew of someone looking for a position.[4] If no response was forthcoming, she turned to the daily newspapers, just as women do today, either by checking printed ads placed by prospective servants looking for positions or by inserting a notice in the papers herself, indicating that she needed general household help.[5]

Registering with one of a number of servants' registry offices (employment agencies) operating in London was another alternative.[6] Some of these registers were offshoots of charitable institutions; through them a housewife could often get untrained but amenable orphan girls from the workhouses.[7] The Metropolitan Association for Befriending Young Servants, for one, founded in London in 1875 to place poor women and children as domestics, handled thousands of applications of girls looking for positions after 1880.[8] The Girl's Friendly Society, a similar institution, which had registration offices throughout London, claimed processing almost 2,000 applications in 1885 alone.[9]

The others were private registries. These unfortunately suffered dubious reputations, having been known to exploit both the girls looking for employment and matrons seeking help, and the latter were regularly warned against their possible shady practices.[10] (In fact, efforts to police the profession met with such little success that compulsory government licensing of employment registries was finally instituted early in the twentieth century.)[11]

Eventually a prospective servant would come before the new housewife for an interview, bearing in hand letters of reference from her previous employers known as a "character" (although if a girl came with no prior experience, such a reference would be nonexistent).[12] Although household manuals routinely warned matrons that these documents were sometimes forged, suggesting that before they did any hiring, they should also interview the servant's former mistress (and in person)[13]; it is doubtful whether the newly married woman did so thorough a screening. Desperate for help, she was in no position to be choosy.

Finding a suitable maid-of-all-work, in the end, probably was a matter of trial and error.

Unfortunately for both the housewife and the maid-of-all-work, the job involved rather unpleasant conditions of work. The hours were long: often from 6:30 A.M. to bedtime, which could be 10 or even 11 P.M. The work was hard, as explained in the previous chapter, involving mopping or scrubbing floors, beating or sweeping carpets, brushing down draperies, running up and down stairs to tote and fetch, scrubbing clothes on washboards with harsh soaps, wringing them out and hanging them up to dry, starching and ironing the clothes—being on one's feet all day long. Amenities were minimal. The servant's bedroom was generally small, dimly lit, poorly heated, and not well ventilated, situated in the attic or on the top floor—and never available for a midday rest.[14]

The maid-of-all-work's diet, although much improved from servants' fare earlier in the century, was generally inadequate (though not intentionally so), considering the amount of energy she expended on the job. And for all this, the going wage, in 1875, in addition to room and board, was from £6 to £15 per annum, although in later years, the range rose to £12 to £28.[15]

Of course, these conditions often were no worse than what the servant had known at home or at a previous position.[16] Still the job had many unattractive features that were immediately evident, overriding whatever initial attractions such a position seemed to hold out to the candidate.

The housewife could do nothing about the amount or nature of the work the general servant was asked to do, since she could not afford hiring a second servant to spread out the work load. For the same reason, she could not pay the servant a higher wage.[17] Moreover, since the housewife often worked alongside her maid-of-all-work, and just as long and hard, she was not inclined to be sympathetic when the maid complained about the drudgery.

The only feature the housewife could have changed was to offer more amenities: a pleasanter bedroom, permission for the girl to have "off time" when she wasn't "on call," or greater leniency regarding food snacks or visits from friends. But the housewife could acquire this kind of flexibility only through experience of being an employer, and it would be many years, if ever, before she would see the servant problem from the viewpoint of the domestic rather than her own.[18]

If hiring was difficult, training the girl was even more so—and at this point friction and tension between the housewife and her servant surfaced. Unlike matrons in wealthier households, the housewife had no housekeeper to act as a go-between in dealing with the less-skilled servants; she had to face the help directly.[19] It was a difficult learning experience for them both. The mistress had to learn how to give orders and supervise without intimidating, teaching the girl how to do what was expected of her. The servant, for her part, had to learn a new kind of work discipline, complying with middle-class procedures and standards of cleanliness that were completely foreign to her.[20]

Domestic manuals and women's magazines, which readily doled out advice to the housewife on how to handle her servants, had a tendency to blame the housewife for friction between servant and employer, and items on the advice-givers' list of employer deficiencies were explicit: she was not taking a personal interest in her servants, she was not making them "real friends," she was not giving them good books and newspapers to read as ways to improve themselves.[21] On the other hand, considering the age and nature of maids-of-all-work, this censure may have been misplaced. The servant usually came from a background of extreme poverty, either a laborer's cottage or the slums of the city; had no experience whatever with what the middle class considered to be the normal, ordinary habits of civilized life; and was very young—almost half of the general servants being under twenty years of age.[22] It is unlikely that the girl could even read. Under such circumstances and considering the housewife's own inexperience, admonitions to give one's servant "kindly advice and support" hardly helped the housewife cope with what she felt, with great frustration, was the root of the problem: the domestic's incompetence.

More often than not, the first girl hired eventually left. Usually she was dismissed because the housewife felt she was unwilling or unable to learn middle-class methods and standards, although sometimes she was let go for dishonesty; but just as often, the servant left on her own accord for a position elsewhere which promised higher pay or a job of greater status than mere housecleaning.[23] Then the hiring and training process would begin all over again.

The second servant the housewife was to hire was either a cook or a nursemaid to help take care of the children. If the children came fairly early in the marriage and if the matron did not mind being cook (or did not mind it as much as she did the chores that were involved in caring for the babies and toddlers), the second servant surely was a nursemaid. For the housewife, the nursemaid had two sterling qualities to recommend her: she could be paid less than a cook and was far less independent.

As will be explained in a later chapter, the middle-class mother of 1875 wanted to become directly involved with the care and upbringing of her children, certainly more than her mother had done in the previous generation and certainly far more than did the upper-middle-class or upper-class women of her own generation, who relied, for the most part, on nannies to raise their children.

The middle-class woman of moderate means did not choose to hire a nanny for a number of reasons. In some cases, she was afraid that the children might pick up unsuitable habits if they were in the constant company of this servant-in-charge. She had been warned, for example, that a nanny might have a distinctive dialect that the children would pick up, or might use strong language, or even drink.[24] She far preferred someone, such as a nursemaid, who would work under her (the mother's) supervision and not actually take charge of the nursery. The housewife looked on the nursemaid as a servant to do the menial nursery chores such as cleaning up after the children, feeding and helping to dress them, lighting fires, and carrying the hot water and meals up and down the stairs to and from the nursery.[25] These were the unpleasant jobs of child-caring that the mother did not want to do.[26]

Never as well trained nor as well paid as a nanny, the nursemaid was closer in age and experience on the job (or lack of it) to the general servant—and in many cases when the family could only afford one servant, she *was* the general servant, child-minding being just part of her job.[27] Her recruitment, training, and position in the household was identical to that of the maid-of-all-work, and unfortunately her tenure was often just as short; in a survey done at the end of the century, one-third to one-half of all the nursemaids in London were found to have been in the same household for less than a year, with the average length of service in a single household being fifteen months for four-fifths of the servants.[28] When the nursemaid left, the housewife had to start recruiting once more.

Hiring a cook, the alternative second servant in the household, was not exactly a variation on the "general servant" or "nursemaid" theme; other factors were introduced that made the hiring and retaining of a cook a problem of a different order.

In theory there were two kinds of cooks available for hire: "plain" or "professed."[29] The former was only capable of preparing plain, familiar English food that the family would eat the year around, but the latter professed to be able to turn out an elegant dinner of six, eight, or ten courses as demanded by the entertaining hostess.[30] However, since a professed cook commanded a wage of £45 per annum,[31] the probability of such a cook working for a family of moderate means was not great. Nor was it likely that *any* cook hired in this middle-class home could have prepared the fancy French cuisine Mrs. Beeton suggested for formal dinner parties. In fact, most cooks were not schooled in their trades at all; most learned by and large on the job. There were no training schools for cooks until 1860, when a cookery school was opened in London to teach professed cookery to servants.[32] Even when, in the 1880s, a number of cooking schools opened in London, there never were enough schools to make much difference in standards of cooking.[33]

Though it seems likely that this middle-class housewife was only looking for a plain cook, the hiring process was more difficult, more tension-filled, than that of hiring other domestics. Because the cook commanded a higher wage, was of higher status, was older (even than the housewife herself) and less easily intimidated than the other servants in the household, the housewife sensed that she was somewhat at a disadvantage. More important, she was acutely aware, based on what she read and was told by others, that a correct decision on the woman's character and qualifications had to be made at the moment of hiring. She would not have leisure to reconsider or modify her decision once it was made. As proved to be the case, once the cook was hired and installed in the kitchen, the servant "held her mistress's reputation in the hollow of her ladle and both of them knew it."[34] The cook's good behavior and performance became so essential to the smooth operation of the house that the housewife found she had to regularly overlook less-than-satisfactory behavior in order to avoid unpleasantness or possible culinary calamity, and was forced to grant many privileges to the cook that she would have preferred not to have done.

The most sensitive point of contention was not wages but perquisites. One privilege most often demanded by the cook was the right to sell the household drippings to dealers and keep the profits[35]—although the housewife would have far preferred that the drippings be used in the cooking to make the roasts more palatable. Another was the cook's insistence on dealing with the tradespeople herself,[36] not because she was particularly concerned by the quality or price of the food but because the commission paid to her by the favored vendors was a custom-recognized addition to her income to which she felt she was entitled.[37] Still another was her insistence that she be allowed to work without interference from the mistress.[38] This demand, however, trespassed greatly on the housewife's authority, and in this instance cook did not always get her way.

While these points of friction were not always evident when the cook was hired, they were certain to arise sooner or later. Trying to find a balance between the interests of cook that she might permit and those which she could not was very stressful for the housewife. More often than not, when the cook's behavior became too embarrassing to be tolerated or her cooking failures too frequent to be ignored, the housewife reluctantly dismissed her, and the hiring process was begun all over again.

In the final analysis, whether the housewife was looking to

hire a general servant, a nursemaid, or a cook, the root of the problem was simple economics. For the wages and working conditions offered, the only domestic who applied, was hired, and stayed on the job was just barely competent. By the turn of the century, the middle-class housewife would come to realize, in exasperation, that the only answer to the servant problem lay in simplifying her housekeeping chores, getting a house that was more efficient for her purposes, and accumulating enough mechanical labor-saving devices so that she could manage her house by herself and do away with live-in servants entirely.[39]

NOTES

1. White, *Women's Magazines*, 54.
2. Ibid., 55.
3. Horn, *The Victorian Servant*, 24–25.
4. Davidson, *Book of the House*, vol. 3, 2–3.
5. Ibid., 3–4.
6. Ibid., 3.
7. Ibid.
8. Theresa M. McBride, *The Domestic Revolution: The Modernization of Household Service in England and France, 1820–1920* (New York: Holmes & Meier, 1976), 77; also Turner, *What the Butler Saw*, 243.
9. Horn, *The Victorian Servant*, 41–42.
10. *Dickens's Dictionary of London*, 244.
11. Turner, *What the Butler Saw*, 243.
12. Branca, *Silent Sisterhood*, 56.
13. Ibid., 31.
14. McBride, *Domestic Revolution*, 51.
15. Beeton, *Book of Household Management*, 16.
16. As Nicholas Bentley noted (*The Victorian Scene*, 230), "All the same it was decidedly better than sleeping seven in a room on a straw mattress in a damp cottage, rising at dawn and working for eleven hours, gleaning or hoeing turnips."
17. McBride, *Domestic Revolution*, 50.
18. Ibid.

19. Ibid., 19.
20. Ibid., 28.
21. Panton, *From Kitchen to Garrett*, 154, 155, 159.
22. Branca, "Image and Reality," 187.
23. Davidson, *A Woman's Work*, 170.
24. Ibid.
25. Ibid.
26. McBride, " 'As the Twig Is Bent,' " 51.
27. Ibid.
28. Data drawn from C. Collet, "Money Wages of In-Door Domestic Servants, Parliamentary Papers, 1899, XCII," 13; as reproduced and quoted in McBride, " 'As the Twig Is Bent,' " 50.
29. Turner, *What the Butler Saw*, 133.
30. Ibid., 133–34.
31. Wilson, *Life in a Victorian House*, 7.
32. Huggett, *Life Below Stairs*, 101.
33. Ibid.
34. Turner, *What the Butler Saw*, 134.
35. Ibid., 136.
36. Ibid., 134.
37. Ibid.
38. Ibid.
39. Davidson, *A Woman's Work*, 176. With the dearth of housemaids late in the century, she drew up a similar list.

CHAPTER 8

The Housewife as Financial Manager: Balancing the Budget

Managing family finances, like handling the servants, was a function the middle-class married woman learned on the job, but in this case it was something about which she had neither prior knowledge nor experience before she married. Moreover, managing the money in the Victorian household, as perhaps is true today, gave rise to anxieties of a special kind. Very often the housewife found she had responsibilities that required the spending of money that she did not actually have in hand, and many times she had to make choices between spending alternatives when it was not clear whether or not she had the authority to make a choice at all.

At the beginning of the woman's marriage, money management was not a problem to her because her financial responsibilities were limited. The only financial matter that concerned the middle-class housewife in 1875, according to the writers of the domestic manuals, was learning how to keep a detailed account of how she spent the food allowance her husband gave her. Mrs. Beeton's *Book of Household Management* told the housewife to procure a housekeeping account book (to be found at any stationery store) and list in it all expenditures she made, "punctually and precisely,"[1] first as a daily diary of purchases, later transferred into separate tradesmen's accounts (i.e., the butcher, the baker, etc.).[2] Ostensibly this was to guard against dishonesty by the tradesmen[3]—although an implicit reason seemed to be that exercising meticulous accounting practices was in general a good habit for a housewife to acquire.[4]

It is not clear, however, whether the housewife actually paid the bills at all. Domestic manuals often spoke as though the housewife always had cash on hand to pay her bills promptly,[5] but often the same books, when writing in a different context but about the same period, stated that tradespeople automatically sent the bills each month (or sometimes at longer intervals, even up to once a year) directly to the man of the house, who in due course paid them.[6] The housewife perhaps was given a household allowance in actual coins, money which she could disperse herself, but she certainly did not have enough money to pay for large bulk purchases of supplies such as candles or soap (urged on her by the domestic economy experts)[7]; this surely would have been the husband's prerogative.

During the twenty-five years of the marriage, however, the woman's role in the management of household expenditures became more complicated. Partly it may have been due to a shift in middle-class attitudes that saw marriage as a partnership, with an increased role for the wife in a "mutual sharing of family governance."[8] More probably, it was directly related to economic changes in the marketplace, particularly relating to retail distribution.

During the last quarter of the nineteenth century, a new type of retail shop, the department store, was seen more and more frequently on the high streets of city and suburb, attracting shoppers with its wide assortment of merchandise, many customer amenities, competitive prices, and the attractive display of goods. In addition to these innovations, the stores instituted a number of novel selling policies, one in particular running counter to earlier retailing precepts: the requirement that all purchases be paid for in cash.[9]

To take advantage of the department store's many attractive goods and services, the middle-class housewife had to carry cash with her when she went shopping and in amounts far, far greater than just her ordinary food allowance.

The matter of cash-handling by the middle-class housewife in the late decades of the nineteenth century is somewhat obscure, with large gaps in our understanding of the way money was transferred in the consumer sector. For example, while check-writing was universally accepted for business transactions in England by the mid-nineteenth century,[10] it is not clear whether checks were actually written (and accepted) for consumer purchases—and, if they were, when and whether the housewife ever wrote them. Were checks regarded as "cash" in the department stores (i.e., as opposed to "buying on credit"), when the stores requested cash on purchase? Did the matron have a bank account against which she could write checks over her signature (as women in America did[11]) for purchases at a department store?

If not, how did she pay for large purchases? As more and more of the family clothing allowance was spent on cloth that the housewife herself sewed into garments, how did she buy the costly yard goods? Did her husband give her the actual cash (a sizable sum) to take to the department store? When, if ever, did she acquire full jurisdiction over clothing expenditures by paying the bills herself?

How did she pay for the really expensive goods, such as household appliances or replacement furniture, for sale in the department store? If her husband did not give her such large sums of cash, did he have to accompany her every time she went shopping so he could pay out the money required?

The same questions asked about the payment of goods must be asked about paying for services, such as servants' wages. How were the servants paid and, more important, *who* paid the servants in the 1880s and 1890s? Did the husband literally hand them their quarterly wages? Or did the housewife eventually get fiscal as well as directional control over the servants? If so, when?

With regard to upkeep of the house, if a woman's responsibility included attention to such maintenance jobs as cleaning the flues, periodic outside-window washing, cleaning the roof eaves, or pruning in the garden; who contracted for, hired, and paid the outside workmen? Was it she or her husband?

Further discussion of spending in the family leads directly to the matter of income budgeting: outgo must equal income. Yet in the area of budgeting, too, ambiguities of responsibility and jurisdiction abound.

The domestic manuals discussed budgeting as though it was based on decisions by the housewife alone.[12] They made no mention of the husband at all, even though it is clear that, in even the most permissive family, the man's role must have been considerable. Since budgeting involved income and outgo, with the husband earning the money from which expenditures were made, one must presume that many husbands felt that budgeting of *their* earnings fell clearly within their jurisdiction.

In any case, the domestic manual writers all regarded budgeting as a rational process, simply a chart-making matter involving the allocation of various amounts of the family income into devised categories. Their pages abounded with suggested budgetary formulas.

As an example, one sample budget offered as a guideline for a family slightly larger than that of our MCMW's, with an income similar to, perhaps slightly smaller than her husband's, appeared in the 1874 edition of John Walsh's *Manual of Domestic Economy*.[13] Mr. Walsh's budget strategy was simple. He divided the family income, first, into large, inclusive categories: one-half of the money for the supplies of the house (including food), one-eighth for rent and taxes, one-eighth for clothing, one-eighth for illness and amusement, and one-eighth for wages of servants, incidental expenses, and charities. Then these broad categories were broken down into smaller divisions. In specific pounds and shillings, this was the printed budget that he devised:

1. **Food**			
Bread	£12		
Milk, butter, cheese	10		
Grocery	10		
Greengrocery	8		
Butcher's meat	30		
Wine, spirits	1		
Beer	8	£79	
Chandlery (candles and soap)		3	
Washing		3	£85
2. **Rent and Taxes**			£17 10s.
3. **Clothing**			£17 10s.
4. **Servants' wages, incidental expenses, and charities**			£10
5. **Illness, amusements**			£10
Total			£150

Hardly an income distribution that allowed much leeway for untoward expenditures! Still, with only the newlywed couple and one or two servants in the household, this budgeting plan would have provided a simple guide for the housewife to follow, particularly if the wife had only food money to allocate, with her spouse in charge of everything else.

Twenty-five years later, the budgeting picture was both different and very much more complicated, not only because the kinds and range of expenditures had changed but because of the change in the way goods from the department stores were now paid for, as explained earlier in the chapter.

In 1901, another sample budget appeared in *Cornhill Magazine* in an article that was one of a series on budgeting for various incomes. This particular article was written by G. S. Layard—but as an addendum to the article, the magazine editor printed a budget to cover a family of two adults, two children, and one servant with an income of £250 per annum,[14] analogous to the finances of the MCMW's family twenty-five years into her marriage. When adjusted so that the categories fit the five Walsh categories of 1874, the editor's budget read as follows:

1. **Food and supplies of the house:**
   Food and housekeeping expenses   £90
   Breadwinner's lunches and teas in
     town   £30   £120

2. **Household-related expenses:**
   Rent and Taxes   £33
   Season railway ticket (third class)* £4 10s.
   Coal and gas (gas cooking stove)   £7 10s.
   Repairs, additions to furniture   £4   £49

3. **Clothing**   £17 10s.

4. **Servants wages, incidental expenses, charities:**
   Servants' wages   £12
   Life, fire insurance premiums   £10 5s.
   Church-sittings, small subscriptions £3 5s.   £25 10s.

5. **Illness & Amusements**
   Doctors   £3
   Holidays   £12
   Sundries (recreational bus fares,
     garden, newspaper, magazines,
     books, postage, presents,
     volunteering, etc.)   £10   £25

                  Total   £237

*This train ticket for the husband to go to work and return each day was regarded as part of the rent because it was only due to his commuting that the family was able to live in the suburbs, paying low rent.

When the two budgets are compared, the first being the one the newlyweds could have followed in 1875 and the second to fit the family twenty-five years later, the revealed differences are significant.

Between 1875 and 1900, the cost of food had fallen substantially[15] so that the amount allocated for food at the end of the century was the same as in 1874, even though the number of dependents was larger, family entertainment was more frequent and on a more lavish scale, and out-of-home food expenses were included.

The amount allocated for clothing remained identical. Cheap ready-made clothing and shoes had, by the later decades, flooded the market (thanks to the introduction of the industrial sewing machine),[16] and savings were passed on by the producers and the retailing outlets as lower costs to the consumers.[17] Coupled with the housewife's ready use of the domestic sewing machine, the family dressed better and more fashionably at the same cost.[18]

Other costs increased. The cost of housing rose continuously and appreciably throughout the century, even in the suburbs. By 1900, housing-related expenses (which included household utilities, repair to the house, and replacement of worn-out furniture previously ignored) accounted for over 20 percent of the budget.[19]

Servants' wages had also greatly increased, each servant being paid perhaps a third more in 1901 than in the early 1870s,[20] and more servants were on the staffs. In addition, the hidden costs of feeding and lodging the servants, uncalculated costs added onto the wages paid out, also had risen proportionately,[21] though not reflected in the 1901 sample budget. Servants' wages and costs became the second largest item in the budget of many middle-class households.[22]

New items appeared in the later budget not considered in 1874, such as life and fire insurance. Also the amounts set aside for religious participation and charitable contributions, and for living amenities such as newspapers, magazines and books, gardens, going on holiday, and so forth rose. In 1874, the amount set aside for amusements was negligible, but by century's end, this category had expanded to include new forms of recreation now regarded as essential and highly valued by the couple and their children. What earlier in the century had been a luxury had by the last decades become a necessity, bringing about a major shift in the family's spending pattern.

The really huge expenses for the middle-class family, inexplicably omitted from both sample budgets, were the costs of raising children. Medical expenses increased as more children survived than earlier in the century and as middle-class parents called in doctors more readily when illness struck. But the prime priority in spending for children was in education.

Middle-class parents now saw that their sons faced greater competition for good employment positions in industry and commerce, requiring a more formal education for the boys.[23] In these later years, it was often seen as essential that the boys go to a recognized grammar or private day school.[24]

In the later decades, educating girls was also considered important (though of course not as important as educating boys), and sending them to one of the new type of schools in London, the Girls Public Day School Trust foundations,[25] required tuition. In addition, because children were dependent for a longer time, their formal training had to be continued for a longer period and for all the children, raising the cost of education significantly.

Not incidentally, the relationship of the number of children to the cost of education was not lost on the late-nineteenth-century middle class. Well-regarded present-day researchers feel that deliberate family limitation had its origin in this class in the 1870s and 1880s, the trend toward a smaller-size family being initiated by the desire of late Victorian middle-class parents to launch a lesser number of children more successfully in life.[26]

Both of the budgets given were constructed by men. It is possible that this method of budgeting expenditures, that is, by constructing charts with simply labeled categories, is how the Victorian middle-class man would have drawn up a budget for his family.

Paper budgeting, while interesting, probably did not occupy the middle-class married woman's attention when thinking of the family's financial problems. Unless spending the family income in the real world was substantially different in late Victorian years than in middle-class households twenty, fifty, or even one hundred years later; budgeting by chart-making was not the way it was done.

The housewife probably budgeted the family income (if indeed it was her prerogative to do) in an *ad hoc* manner, shifting the tentative categories about as various needs arose in a method that domestic manual writers thoroughly discouraged! By amalgamating money management with budgeting strategy, she would have worked out a procedure, with her husband's consent, as to which of the two would paid for what, and how actual money was transferred from his hands into hers.

In general, unless the housewife was especially acute in financial matters or influenced by the exhortations of the New Women whose views frequently appeared in domestic women's magazines, she was not particularly anxious to become the hands-on money manager. Who handled the money was not important to her unless it impinged on authority she felt was hers to exercise. Therefore, most of her money managing was covert, with her requesting rather than demanding, cajoling instead of asserting, making do where she had to while insisting on more leeway when she felt the family welfare (or her own prerogatives) required it. She probably did a lot of creative maneuvering with the family finances.

An initial problem, one that was true fifty years later and perhaps even today, was that the housewife never knew exactly what her husband's income was or how much of it was hers to spend. The man may possibly have mentioned to his wife the amount of his take-home pay, but not necessarily. Since one's precise income was closely related to status and thus tended to be a touchy subject, he may have been reticent to go into specifics. Still, it probably didn't matter because the woman could deduce her husband's salary by the food and clothing allowances he gave her. According to the magazines that she read, these were fairly stable percentages of annual income.

The following then, although conjecture, may closely resemble the way the late-Victorian London matron budgeted the income and handled the family expenditures.

Budgeting would have been a pragmatic affair: making sure money was on hand for all absolutely necessary expenditures while juggling the rest of the money to put aside and cover what was left. All expenditures, thus, fell into three general categories.

The first included the hard, "must pay" expenses, costs that were known and inflexible, such as rent and servants' wages. These did not vary and always had to be paid at designated quarterly intervals.

The second category also included "must pay" costs that were known, but the amounts were flexible rather than inflexible, such as money to be spent on clothing for the entire family. This expenditure could be put off for a while, but eventually had to be made.

The final grouping was the catch-all, "everything else" category of disposable income, as amorphous as it was vital. It included all things that were necessary to make a better life for her and for her family, in amounts yet unknown, to be paid out at irregular intervals, for needs that were not yet defined.

Knowing in general what her husband's income was, the housewife made it her responsibility to see that money was always there to pay for the "musts."

The fixed, inflexible items in the budget included rent,

taxes, the cost of her husband's transportation to and from work, the cost of utilities (coal and gas), and fire and life insurance: a known number of pounds per year. The bills for these big items were paid for by her husband (she would have decided); whether by check or by cash was of no concern to her.

Servants' wages were also a fixed, inflexible expenditure, but as the century drew to a close she may have insisted that the time had come for *her* to pay the servants, not him. Paying the servants' wages was one way, she saw, to buttress her control and authority over them. This category swelled in time to also include the wages of temporary help which had risen as she, the housewife, cut back on her own housecleaning and laundering work: the washerwomen, the yard- and handy men, and the occasional front-room servants for special-occasion dinner parties.

Money for food was a flexible budget item (since it could vary from week to week), but a tangible one in that she had to have the actual cash in her possession to order to pay for purchases. In that sense, it was a fixed item whose outlay could not be postponed. Since food accounted for about half of the family income, it was a large amount of money, but as a budgeted category, it was no different than the food allowance she had had control over for her entire marriage.

Similarly, the clothing item was also a flexible but tangible expense. Part of it was not under her control at all; it was spent by her husband to purchase his own made-to-order clothing from his tailor, bootmaker, and haberdasher before he gave her the clothing allowance. What was left was under her control, as it had been from the beginning of their marriage.

The disposable income made up the "catch-all" category. Unfortunately, much of the disposable income was also encumbered, that is, it was money to be set aside for anticipated but required one-time needs. From this set-aside money, for example, all emergency medical and nursing expenses that unexpectedly arose had to be taken. Also from this pool, money had to be found (and a lot of it) to pay for the children's formal education as they grew older. How much had to be put aside depended on whether the children were boys or girls and how many of each, whether free schools were available or acceptable, whether day rather than boarding schools were available or acceptable, and on the number of years education would be required.

A fixed item in the "catch-all" category but of unspecified quantity was money earmarked to replace worn-out (to her way of thinking) furniture and furnishings and to purchase new household labor-saving devices coming on the market, such as a gas stove to replace the old coal range, or an improved sewing machine for machine-stitching the fancy accoutrements and decorations that previously had to be hand-sewn. At the beginning of their marriage, this item was postponable and possibly superfluous, but as the years passed, it was upgraded to a necessary item to be paid out sooner rather than later. However, these purchases, large in size and money, probably were considered as expenditures that could be handled on a hire-purchase (installment) plan. Despite the almost unanimous disapproval of all domestic advice-giving experts, buying on the installment plan was a real and useful tool used by middle-class families of moderate means to pay for the large items they needed.[27]

Money from this "leftover" disposable-income fund also paid for family recreation and entertainment, a growing expenditure as the children grew older and as the social circles in which the woman and her husband traveled expanded. Finally, not yet fully articulated but considered for the first time since her marriage, the middle-class married woman contemplated using an as-yet-undetermined portion of the family income for her own personal needs and pleasure.

As the century drew to its close, budgeting the family income became more and more difficult. It had to accommodate not only progressively escalating expenses, but rising expectations—things the housewife hoped for but of which her mother never dreamed. The problem was not a matter of keeping accurate records of expenses, as the domestic manuals kept insisting. The problem was, simply and as always, that there was not enough income to offset the perceived expenditures.

Because this budget imbalance was persistent—as acute (if not more so) in 1900 as it was in 1875—it served to feed the middle-class woman's anxiety and discontent, leading her to cast about for solutions. What she eventually did, as will be later detailed, had widespread ramifications.

NOTES

1. Beeton, *Book of Household Management*, 6.
2. Ibid.
3. Branca, *Silent Sisterhood*, 26.
4. Ibid.
5. Ibid., 28.
6. Mrs. Beeton (*Book of Household Management*, 32), states that the housekeeper not only must keep an accounting of all expenses, whether in cash or credit, but she must always check on bills sent in by tradespeople, thus indicating that not all bills were paid for in cash. Also, see Sally Mitchell (*Victorian Britain*, 720), who notes that goods were often purchased without money changing hands; bills were submitted monthly by market tradespeople.
7. Branca, *Silent Sisterhood*, 28.
8. Ibid., 123.
9. Adburgham, *Shops and Shopping*, 720.
10. E. Victor Morgan, *A History of Money* (Baltimore: Penguin Books, 1965), 27.
11. Explained in detail in C. W. Haskins' *How to Keep Household Accounts: A Manual of Family Finance* (New York: Harper & Bros., 1902). Obviously written for an American audience, there seems some question as to whether or not it pertained as well to the British housewife.
12. Branca, *Silent Sisterhood*, 26–28.

13. John Walsh's budgeting provisions are detailed in Branca, *Silent Sisterhood*, 28.

14. G. S. Layard, "Family Budgets: A Lower-Middle-Class Budget," in *Cornhill Magazine*, N.S., 10 (1901), 666.

15. Burnett, *Cost of Living*, 214.

16. Jefferys, *Retail Trading*, 8.

17. Burnett, *Cost of Living*, 214.

18. Ibid., 215.

19. As indicated in the *Cornhill Magazine* budget, noted in text.

20. Horn, *The Victorian Servant*, 24.

21. McBride, *Domestic Revolution*, 50.

22. Burnett, *Cost of Living*, 240.

23. Ibid., 243–44.

24. Ibid., 244.

25. Ibid.

26. J. A. Banks and Olive Banks, *Feminism and Family Planning in Victorian England* (Liverpool: Liverpool University Press, 1964), 13.

27. Branca, *Silent Sisterhood*, 28–29.

CHAPTER 9

The Housewife in Her Maternal Role: As Bride, Potential Mother, and Pregnant Wife

Up to now, we have considered the middle-class married woman in terms of her daily preoccupation as "housewife." In asking "What did she do all day?" we looked into the various tasks she assumed on her own initiative as part of the daily routine.

Now we broaden the perspective and look to see how the middle-class married woman handled responsibilities which, while part of the implicit marital contract, were not routines in which she actually did things; in fact, they were often activities in which she played a passive rather than an active role. The next few chapters will ask, not "What did she do?" but "What did she do about . . . ?" The answers are as revelatory as were those that explained the tasks she did in her diurnal rounds.

Our young middle-class girl, as a bride, probably learned about the sexual aspects of marriage in the marital bed chamber on her wedding night. Anecdotal and possibly apocryphal stories of women in early and mid-century Victorian England tell of an ignorance among girls so enormous that betrothed women often made no connection whatsoever between the pleasurable excitement they felt during their engagement and the sexual participation expected of them after they were married. Discovery often was brutal.

While it does not seem possible that this was still true in 1875, who can say? Thirty-five years later, the editor of a woman's magazine remarked that, judging from the letters she received, "ignorance of the obligations, privileges and marvels of married life is as widespread today as it was in the darkest ages of the history of women."[1]

However, once married, the young woman not only discovered but learned to participate in the sexual pleasures of this new union. Contrary to the much-quoted statement of Victorian physician William Acton that females rarely were troubled by sexual feelings,[2] there was open recognition, even as far back as 1825, that sexual enjoyment was often actively sought by women as well as men.[3]

What the bride also learned was that, unfortunately, sexual pleasure led to consequences that were somewhat less rapturous: pregnancy.

One cannot say with any degree of certainty what the bride in 1875 thought about pregnancy (if, when, and how often), family size (large, small, or none at all), and the intentional spacing of children through the deliberate use (and, at intervals, the non-use) of contraceptive devices. Unquestionably, she wanted children: she was no *avant garde*, zero-population advocate like Dr. Elizabeth Blackwell, who in 1870 stated that children were not at all necessary for a successful marriage.[4] Because of her upbringing, our bride saw motherhood as one of a woman's most fulfilling functions.[5]

On the other hand, as a modern woman (in her own eyes), she must have felt ambivalence about the consequences of her mother's repeated, closely spaced pregnancies, witnessed as a member of a large family herself. It is likely that she knew of her mother's childbearing ordeals, in pain, suffering, and simply exhaustion, and was aware of the lack of amenities in the family, directly caused by the necessity of providing for so many children on a very limited income.

More than that, she could not help knowing, and being understandably frightened about, the real danger of dying during childbirth or immediately afterwards. Personal knowledge of the demise of relatives, family friends, and neighbors could not have been avoided. Maternal mortality rates had not subsided in the later years of the century as might have been expected. Statistics show that in 1892, the rate of maternal mortality had hardly changed from what it was fifty-five years earlier, being 4.9 to every 1,000 births in 1892 as compared to 5 in every 1,000 births in 1838.[6] Equally frightening to one who saw each child as a precious thing was the equally high infant mortality that took place within the child's first year of life (as will be discussed in a later chapter).

While the young bride vaguely knew there were techniques for limiting the size of the family, she could not have been very sophisticated about learning ways of preventing pregnancy. It is possible that, before she could straighten out her own thinking on the matter and bring herself to talk to her husband about this delicate subject, she had already become pregnant. (In 1874 a study of middle-class families showed that more than 80 percent recorded the birth of a child within the first year of marriage.)[7]

The first year of marriage was a crucial one in all respects. While still adjusting to the sexual aspects of her life and to the possible and still equivocal prospect of becoming a mother, the young bride probably came to some understanding with her husband on family size: how many children they really wanted, how that number would be distributed throughout her childbearing years and, most crucial, how to prevent unwanted pregnancies. Getting pregnant inadvertently would be a mistake she and her husband hoped not to make or, if it had already happened, would not repeat a second time.

One of the most intriguing phenomena that occurred during the last quarter of the nineteenth century was the precipitous drop in the size of the family in Great Britain. Census figures show that the birth rate fell from a high of nearly 35.5 births per 1,000 in the 1870s to about 29 per 1,000 by 1900, a drop of more than 21 percent in one generation.[8] During a twenty-five-year span, a major change in attitude toward fecundity obviously took place in all classes throughout the country; it certainly did within London's middle-class.

Historians and social scientists have offered various explanations for this sharp drop in the birth rate. One explanation saw it as a consequence of the Charles Bradlaugh–Annie Besant trial of 1877–78, which prompted their deliberate publication of a 1832 book, Charles Knowlton's *Fruits of Philosophy*, giving explicit birth-control information.[9] Because of the trial, Knowlton's book was reissued and saw the unprecedented sale of 125,000 copies in the late 1870s,[10] making birth control information readily available for the first time to middle-class married women who had before never known how contraception worked.[11]

Another explanation of the drop in the birth rate related to the economics of a rising standard of living. The authors of this theory claim that prosperity and conditions of material well-being had become so important to the middle class that limiting the number of children represented a popular determination to maintain the improved living standards.[12]

Still another explanation was put forth in a twentieth-century government report on population, which looked back over the 1875–1900 period and saw the shrinkage in the size of the family due to multiple causation, with no fewer than seven complicated explanations as factors in the drop in the birth rate.[13]

Perhaps in response to the repeated admonition of the medical profession that spaced pregnancies were important for the good health of women, substantial evidence in the literature at the time indicated that concern for the well-being of the woman was also an important factor in the deliberate effort to limit family size.[14]

By the very privacy of the sexual act, it is impossible to know what decisions were made, but the statistics are proof that not only were deliberate decisions made about using some form of birth control but that, whatever method they chose, it was *effective*. For this reason, it is unlikely that the two male-initiated methods used throughout history—abstinence and *coitus interruptus*—were responsible for the drop in the birth rate, since there was no appreciable reduction in the size of the family when they *had* been used. Deemed the most popular methods employed by nineteenth-century men, this presumption, according to historian Patricia Branca, was based on the literary myth of the autocratic Victorian husband exercising his male procreative prerogatives on a passive, submissive wife, not on any specific evidence.[15]

In addition, a third birth-control choice, that of engaging in sexual activity only during the "safe" period when a woman could not get pregnant also must be ruled out because of its unreliability; medical knowledge in the nineteenth century did not include what the "safe" period happened to be.[16] And while a fourth alternative, abortion, did increase in the second half of the century, there is a question as to whether or not this was a method of choice for middle-class women.[17] Because abortifacient pills were dangerous and often ineffective, and an operation both dangerous and painful, it seems likely that abortion was used by the middle class only as a last resort when preventive methods failed.[18]

Mechanical contraception appears to have been the method most used. The old but popular method remained the condom, especially after vulcanization of rubber made it durable, reliable, and inexpensive.[19] Even though popularly viewed as a male contraceptive, the role of the woman in its use was, at the very least, cooperative,[20] with one early article, ". . . Some Valuable and Novel Information . . . Exclusively to Married Couples by A Married Man (with Six Children)," giving very specific advice to the woman on how to help the man slip it on at the height of sexual activity.[21]

The birth control methods middle-class women most favored were the so-called "female" contraceptives, which transferred control of preventing pregnancy from the husband to the wife: the sponge, the syringe, the pessary, and the diaphragm. The vaginal sponge and the vaginal syringe were both available early in the century.[22] The vaginal pessary, a metal cervical cap, was introduced in England before the middle of the nineteenth century, but after vulcanization was developed in 1843, the rubber diaphragm replaced it in popularity, being more comfortable to use, more durable and less expensive.[23] Not only was the diaphragm safe and reliable but, according to Dr. Henry Allbutt, a woman could use it without the knowledge of her husband.[24] (It should be noted that Allbutt's book, *The Wife's Handbook*, did not come out until 1882; moreover it is not known whether this side advantage was significant in promoting the diaphragm's use.)

Through advertisements that appeared in women's magazines and health manuals describing these devices and their improved versions, middle-class women were made aware, as never before, of the endless possibilities for birth control readily obtainable on the market.[25]

Whether or not the young woman recognized the symptoms of pregnancy (the cessation of her normal menstrual cycle, morning sickness, breast enlargement) is not clear; in any case, the discovery of her new condition was not necessarily a welcome one, particularly if it occurred within the first year of the marriage. During that first year, the young woman was totally involved in furnishing the house, training her just-hired servant, learning to cook the family meals, sewing clothes, budgeting to make the always-too-small income cover rising expenses, and adjusting to her new husband and the pleasures of marital intimacy. Pregnancy, with its accompanying recurring bouts of illness that drained her energy, complicated all of these activities, particularly the last. Just when an added attraction toward her new husband and her own erotic feelings were evolving, she suddenly found herself deprived of these pleasures as pregnancy took over her life.[26]

During her first pregnancy the woman became acquainted with books on the market directed to the soon-to-be mother. Two extremely popular ones were Dr. Thomas Bull's *Hints to Mothers, for the Management of Health during the Period of Pregnancy and Lying-in Room*, which in 1877 was in its fifteenth edition; and Dr. John Conquest's *Letters to a Mother . . . Embracing the Subjects of Pregnancy, Childbirth,* [and] *Nursing. . . .*[27] In addition, periodicals such as *The British Mother's Magazine* and *The Mother's Friend* addressed themselves to her problems, with organizations such as the London Maternal Association dedicated to bringing mothers together to discuss their common experiences.[28]

Unhappily, the manuals and the magazines often were strong on platitudes and did not offer much constructive advice. While Dr. Allbutt counseled pregnant women to keep healthy by avoiding alcohol, eating plain but nourishing food, avoiding late suppers, getting plenty of exercise and rest, and having regular bowel movements, his only instruction for the woman, if threatened with a miscarriage was: "Call immediately for a doctor"![29]—hardly words to decrease anxiety in the first-time mother.

With her first pregnancy, the young woman also made her initial acquaintance with the medical profession upon which she originally pinned high hopes and subsequently learned had major deficiencies.[30] Although it is not known how many pregnant women got prenatal care from doctors, it appears likely that few consulted a doctor until pregnancy was well along since the fees charged by doctors were high, from 10s. to £2.[31] Some women, in fact, probably went through their pregnancy without seeing a doctor at all. Moreover, the help a pregnant woman could get from a doctor was limited. While there had been a progressive professionalization among doctors, especially in the women-related fields of obstetrics, gynecology, and female-problem surgery,[32] surgical advances aside, medical knowledge of the common female health problems including pregnancy, held by general practitioners, remained meager throughout the entire century.[33]

Although it has often been asserted that middle-class married women preferred using a doctor rather than a midwife when the birth was imminent, there are no data, in fact, indicating how many women were attended by midwives and how many by doctors.[34] One of the reasons given for this preference (if true) was the woman's belief that the doctor would give her chloroform at birth, which midwives did not use. Unfortunately, this was not necessarily true. For years, the British medical establishment resisted the use of chloroform for women during childbirth, long after Queen Victoria proclaimed it a miraculous wonder, having had it administered by her physician during the birth of her eighth child in 1853.[35] Not until the end of the 1870s did doctors admit to possible health benefits for women under their care if they ameliorated the agony of childbirth.[36]

Middle-class women may also have turned to physicians and away from untrained midwives in hopes of getting the most advanced help during this very dangerous time, in order to reduce the possibility of dying in the process. In one sense they were correct in shunning midwives, since midwives had no training in handling abnormal problems such as breech births and were unable to help if birth anomalies or hemorrhaging took place.[37] But women were often proven wrong in thinking that the British medical establishment, despite its advanced medical knowledge, was a viable alternative. As will be detailed in the following chapter, too often doctors inadvertently infected parturient women giving birth in hospitals by carrying contagion from other patients they had attended. Because middle-class women turned to doctors most readily for the best and safest care, middle-class women made up a disproportionately large percentage of women who died from puerperal fever.[38]

It is unclear how our MCMW coped during the nine months in which she was "confined," the euphemism for being pregnant. Many of the descriptions of the mother-to-be as being cosseted and indulged were written by men[39] and, if true, probably were appropriate for wealthier women not directly involved with the chores of housecleaning. It seems more likely that our young pregnant woman continued to act as a domestic and housekeeper, with its many demands on her energy and health, as long as she able, conforming to traditional mores in only one respect: keeping out of the public eye as much as possible. If she became overly exhausted or sick, she surely would have taken to her bed, but it is unclear if anything short of the threat of an actual miscarriage would have overcome her strong reluctance to seek medical help. If she needed help, she may have called upon her sisters or her mother (if they lived close) or, if necessary, hired temporary help to keep the house in order.

The actual process of childbirth in 1875 was not much different for this young woman than when her own mother gave birth. If the child was to be born at home and the time was imminent, a temporary monthly nurse (i.e., the nurse who would assist with the birth and care for the mother and the newborn for a while afterwards) may have been hired. But the fees paid a monthly nurse were high, not including the cost of feeding her and giving her a place to sleep,[40] and it is possible that the services of a monthly nurse would not be seen as essential.

Once regular labor pains began, however, the doctor was summoned. This was the family doctor, not usually a trained obstetrician.[41] Dr. Allbutt described in rather harrowing detail the probable actions of the attending doctor,[42] noting particularly the restrictions of "modesty" on his actions, such as his reluctance to make a visual examination of the fetus's position, his marked preference to delay tactile examination until the moment before birth, his reluctance to use forceps even when it would not have harmed the baby and his refusal to give chloroform during a tedious and painful labor even when he knew it would give his patient relief.[43]

Once the baby was born, the monthly nurse, if one had been engaged, would remain until the mother adjusted to the baby and was able to get up on her own feet.[44] If the birth was uncomplicated and the child was full term and relatively well at birth, all the mother had to do was recover and get on with her life. But in many cases, the situation after birth was not so benign. A discussion of the continued precarious nature of the mother's health as well as that of the newborn is described in the following chapter.

NOTES

1. Editorial comment in *Woman's Own* magazine (1910), as reported in White, *Women's Magazines*, 108.

2. From William Acton's book, *The Functions of the Reproductive Organs . . .* (1862), as alluded to by Branca in *Silent Sisterhood*, 124. Acton's statement, however, was not taken as gospel, not even by the medical community. A book reviewer writing in the *London Medical Review*, September 1862, stated that the claim was not only unphysiological but proven wrong by experience.

3. In Richard Carlile's *Every Woman's Book: Or What Is Love?* (1825), 8, as quoted in Branca, *Silent Sisterhood*, 123.

4. Blackwell, *How to Keep a Household in Health*, 8.

5. Branca, *Silent Sisterhood*, 74. Branca will be quoted fairly extensively in this chapter since, in my opinion, she has demonstrated considerable expertise and insight in this area.

6. Ibid., 81.

7. From Ansell, *On the Rate of Mortality . . . in the Upper and Professional Classes*, Table 8, page 49, as reported in Branca, *Silent Sisterhood*, 74–75.

8. Mitchell, *Victorian Britain*, 618.

9. From John Innes, *Class Fertility Trends*, 1, as reported in Branca, *Silent Sisterhood*, 114–15.

10. Mitchell, *Victorian Britain*, 79.

11. Branca, *Silent Sisterhood*, quoting the supporters of this thesis, 115.

The Housewife in Her Maternal Role

12. The analyses as given in J. A. Banks and Olive Banks, *Prosperity and Parenthood*, 6, are discussed in Branca, *Silent Sisterhood*, 116.

13. From the *Report of the Royal Commission on Population*, vol. 19, 1948–49; see Branca, *Silent Sisterhood*, 115.

14. Ibid., 123.

15. Ibid.

16. Allbutt, in *The Wife's Handbook*, 49, stated that the "safe" period was from five days before the monthly flow until eight days afterwards (though readily admitting this method often failed). But according to Dr. John Conquest, in *Letters to a Mother* (quoted in Branca, *Silent Sisterhood*, 130), this was the time a woman was *most* likely to conceive; "almost universal opinion," he states, sets the most fertile period right after the end of the menstrual period.

17. Branca, *Silent Sisterhood*, 129.

18. Ibid., 130.

19. Ibid., 136.

20. Ibid.

21. Branca quotes extensively from this anonymous source, 137.

22. These are both described in detail in Branca, *Silent Sisterhood*, 131, 133.

23. Ibid., 133.

24. Allbutt, *The Wife's Handbook*, 48.

25. Branca, *Silent Sisterhood*, 135.

26. Ibid, 114. "The middle-class woman's new image of self involved a new sexuality—one of more personal enjoyment. In order to maximize sexual enjoyment, it was necessary to prevent the traditional consequences of sex—pregnancy." One can infer the woman's dismay at being deprived of this new-found enjoyment.

27. Ibid., 76.

28. Ibid.

29. Allbutt, *The Wife's Handbook*, 15.

30. Branca, *Silent Sisterhood*, 77.

31. Ibid., 84.

32. Ibid., 63–64.

33. Ibid., 71.

34. Ibid., 78–79.

35. John Miller, " 'Temple and Sewer': Childbirth, Prudery and

Victoria Regina," in *The Victorian Family: Structure and Stresses*, Anthony S. Wohl, ed. (New York: St. Martin's Press, 1978), 24.
36. Branca, *Silent Sisterhood*, 85–86.
37. Ibid., 78.
38. Ibid., 82.
39. Macqueen-Pope, *Twenty Shillings*, 21–24.
40. Ibid., 25.
41. Ibid., 22.
42. Allbutt, *The Wife's Handbook*, 16–21.
43. Ibid., 21–22.
44. Macqueen-Pope, *Twenty Shillings*, 25.

London Bridge.

The Mansion House and Cheapside.

The Bank of England.

Fleet Street and Ludgate Hill.

Houses of Parliament.

Charing Cross.

The Charing Cross Kitchener gas cooker

An electric-company demonstration
of various electrical appliances, c. 1890.

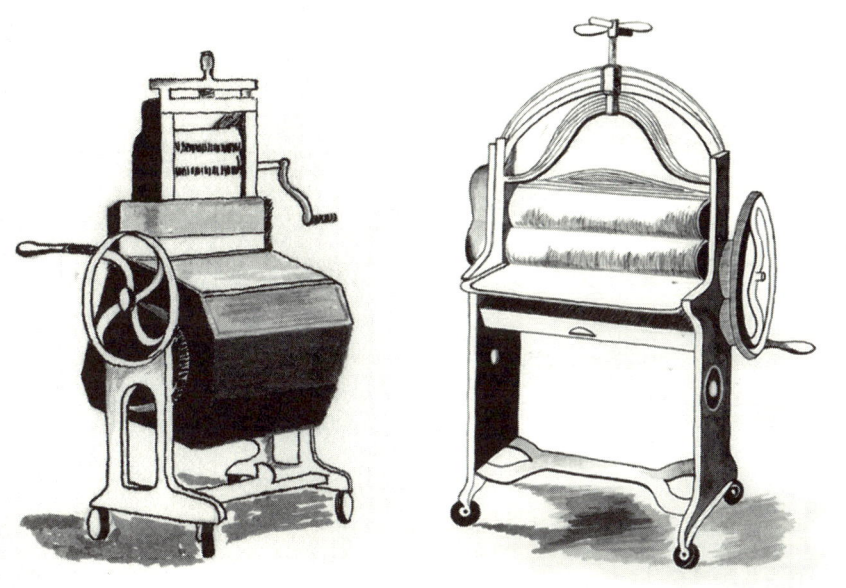

Laundry equipment, c. 1880: hand operated washing machine, wringer-clothes mangle, and box iron.

Furniture and furnishings of the traditional Victorian sitting room, c. 1870-80s.

Traffic on the street in front of Whitely's Department Store, c. 1895.

Woman at her sewing machine, c. 1865. Artwork by Jason Dunda

CHAPTER 10

The Matron as Guardian of the Family's Health

Although the middle-class married woman accepted responsibility for her family's health as part of her sphere of family governance, she had already learned when she gave birth to her first child (and would continue to relearn throughout her married life) that the assurance of good health for her family, the prevention of diseases and ailments that would harm them, and the relief of suffering that illness brought was not in her power to control.

Much of what she wanted for the family and herself, unfortunately, depended on a medical state-of-the-art that was not yet present in 1875, with only minimum progress to be made by the end of the century. Having the money to spend for good medical care or expending vigilance and personal sacrifice when illness struck often had no appreciable effect.

In addition, the frequent unwillingness of medical practitioners to make available what improvements were already known was another problem she had to face. The uneasy story of the British medical establishment's rigid conservatism and its resistance to change in the nineteenth century and the consequences such actions had on the health of the nation cannot adequately be explored here. However, in the case of the housewife who worried about the family's health, her feelings of helplessness in the face of an unwillingness by doctors to pay attention to her concerns or to accept and apply new medical advancements was all too evident.

The struggle for a family's good health began with the good health and stamina of the housewife herself, since she had to be alert and well in order to take care of those around her. We know comparatively little about the general health of the middle-class woman[1]—nor for that matter, of her husband either. We can probably assume they both had fairly hearty constitutions when they were married because, as mentioned: despite diets heavy in fats and lacking in fresh vegetables,[2] they did a great deal of walking throughout their childhood and adolescence.

But once married, the woman's general health probably deteriorated due to the physical demands that the heavy housework involved; most of the time in rooms not properly ventilated or heated. In the early years of marriage, she may have been in a chronic condition of physical exhaustion.[3]

Also, in addition to general health considerations such as diet, exercise regimen, drinking or smoking habits, or genetic tendencies, which operated then as they do today, the Victorians were at the mercy of public health inadequacies such as impure water, the adulteration of food and drink, untreated sewage and improper sanitary arrangements, all of which may have contributed to chronic health problems. Still, London was less susceptible to such public deficiencies than other parts of the country, and the last quarter of the century in particular saw much municipal improvement in these areas.[4]

For the adults, nothing warranted a trip to the doctor in the normal course of events short of catastrophic diseases for which there was no cure, such as tuberculosis ("consumption") or cancer.[5] In cases of middle-class families of low income, the reluctance to see a doctor may have been prompted by the expense involved; the usual cost of a house call from a general practitioner was from 2s. 5d. to 5s.[6] Ordinarily, if the housewife or her husband (or the servants) felt physical symptoms that seemed to need medical correction, they went to the chemist and purchased some patent medicine for relief or a cure.[7]

Women in general were, at that time, susceptible to a number of life-threatening illnesses, the most dangerous being respiratory diseases, the greatest cause of death.[8] Tuberculosis in particular accounted for half of all the deaths in women between age fifteen and thirty-five.[9]

For those women who became mothers, the greatest health hazard was death as a consequence of childbirth.

The danger to the mother's life began immediately after the child was born when she was vulnerable to a virulent septic poisoning known as puerperal fever or "childbed fever." The transmitting agent was usually the attending physician who inadvertently carried the infection to her from his other patients.[10] Probably a disproportionate percentage of women who died from puerperal fever were middle class because they were the ones who turned to doctors, rather than midwives, at the time of childbirth.[11]

The tragedy of the high incidence of puerperal fever was that measures to prevent the infection were known since the early 1800s, yet doctors were slow to routinely follow the known precautions.[12] In 1861 the 4.3 deaths of women per 1,000 live births *increased* in 1881 to 4.8 per 1,000, dropping slightly in 1891, to 4.7, only to rise again in 1901, to 4.8.[13]

While these figures were bad enough in themselves, there was also a strong indication that, in England and Wales, childbed deaths were under-reported throughout the period, probably grossly so until the 1880s, with doctors, midwives, officials of lying-in hospitals and Poor Law guardians all interested in keeping the numbers down.[14] Even as late as 1895, an investigation of 4,000 women whose deaths were attributed to metria, blood poisoning, and hemorrhage found that from one-quarter to one-half of the deaths were actually connected to childbirth.[15]

The middle-class married woman's impotence in getting proper medical care for herself immediately after the birth of a child continued for months after the birth had taken place, this time relating to the child. The problem arose in deciding how the newborn was to be fed; and between the mothers and the doctors, there was a decided difference of opinion.

Middle-class mothers preferred not to breast feed their new babies. In general, they found the process much too exhausting,[16] particularly when they still had a household and possibly other small children to take care of.[17] Moreover, if the mother also suffered from complications such as milk fever, engorged breasts, or cracked nipples, the ordeal was extremely painful as well.[18]

The medical profession, on the other hand, almost universally condemned artificial feeding of infants and mothers who resorted to it; they considered breast feeding as a mother's innate function, a duty both unnatural and medically improper to avoid.[19] Whatever complaints mothers had regarding the strain on their own health were dismissed as merely immaterial temporary discomforts.[20]

However, when doctors condemned bottle-feeding for the sake of the baby, their complaints had merit.

Infant mortality was extremely high in England; in fact, it continued to increase over the years. In 1875, the death rate of infants under one year was "158 per 1,000 [live births] or 4 per 1,000 above the average rate in the 10 years 1861–71."[21] By 1899, the death rate was little better than the 1847 record of 163 deaths in 1,000 live births. About 20 percent of all deaths annually still struck children less than one year old,[22] not only for the country as a whole but the middle class as well.[23]

The medical profession, in general, took no responsibility for the high death rate among the newborns, putting the blame squarely on the mothers for refusing to breast-feed their infants.[24] In the minds of many, mothers who deliberately turned their backs on their "natural function" by choosing to bottle-feed their infants instead of breast-feeding them "were held guilty of virtual infanticide."[25]

Possibly because doctors felt so strongly about the moral imperative of breast-feeding (or perhaps for other reasons not known), they did not routinely instruct new mothers on measures they should take if they insisted on bottle-feeding, such as boiling the milk or sterilizing bottles and nipples to circumvent some of the dangers cow's milk presented.[26]

Cow's milk was a very dangerous food in Victorian Britain. It was regarded as the most widely adulterated food available (in 1887, one-quarter of all milk examined by the Local Government Board in London was seriously adulterated).[27] Up to the twentieth century, it was estimated that ten percent of all milk cows produced tubercular milk.[28] Also, milk was a perfect breeding place for bacteria of all kinds, as it sat around in unhygienic containers, unrefrigerated for hours and even days,[29] before being fed to the baby.

Diarrhea was the greatest health hazard to infants drinking contaminated milk. The infant death rate from diarrheal diseases sharply increased after 1885 and as late as 1899 accounted for approximately a quarter of all infant deaths, the single largest cause of infant mortality.[30] Unfortunately, doctors were not overly concerned with the complex causes of gastrointestinal disease as a medical problem. It was the moral lapse of the mothers that had to be addressed, not the medical health of the child; the high infant death rate was the result.

In the end, middle-class mothers did what they thought best which, in most cases, was opting for artificial feeding. But the accusations that experts heaped upon them when, as too frequently happened, their infants fell ill and sometimes died, must have sorely undermined their faith in knowing how to properly care for their babies.[31]

The middle-class mother's helplessness in the face of illness continued as the infants became toddlers and older. No longer embracing the fatalism of the early nineteenth century regarding the inevitability of some children dying, she viewed each of her children as an individual to whom good health and well being was a birthright never in question.[32] Still, although she constantly sought advice on how to keep them in good health, in the end there was little she could do. Because of the inadequacies of British medicine, medical practitioners often did not know how to combat infectious diseases in children and could passed on nothing to mothers of real help.[33] In fact, some remedies they suggested, as will be seen, may have exacerbated the illnesses.

The diseases most fatal to middle-class children between ages four and fourteen were scarlet fever, measles, whooping cough, smallpox, and diphtheria.[34]

Scarlet fever, an extremely infectious streptococcal infection of the throat, skin, and middle ear, varied in incidence and intensity over the century, 1840–70 being particularly virulent years with 26,000 deaths being reported for 1874 alone.[35] But the disease appeared comparatively mild before 1840 and doctors continued to treat the disease in the later, more virulent period with remedies they decided were sufficient in the early benign years. Their remedies included anti-febrile remedies (i.e., methods of cutting down the fever) such as using substances at the illness's end to produce irritation (blisters) on the skin and vomiting,[36] "general evacuants" (laxatives), and copious bloodletting to check the ulceration of the throat.[37] These methods continued to be administered into the early 1880s.

Because middle- and upper-class parents were the ones who sought out doctors and, on their advice, admitted the children to fever hospitals, their children may have been more subjected to scarlet fever's devastation than the less wealthy. In one particular study in the London fever hospitals during a virulent outbreak in 1890–91, the mortality rate of those treated in the hospital was around 7 percent, about twice the rate of those treated at home.[38]

Diphtheria, like scarlet fever, struck the children of the middle-class and wealthier families particularly hard because, in this case, they drank more milk; it turned out that the bacilli in the droplets caused by sneezing and coughing of infected persons incubated and proliferated rapidly in milk.[39]

Measles, a highly contagious viral disease, was spread by droplet infection or by touch.[40] It was a major child killer in the nineteenth century, particularly in mid-winter when it was associated with cough and influenza.[41]

While smallpox, another viral infection, was a disfiguring disease, it was not regarded as a great killer of preschool-age middle-class children in the last quarter of the century. The discovery of vaccination by Edward Jenner in 1790 had proven to be very effective,[42] so much so that after 1840 compulsory vaccination was required of all children.[43] Unquestionably, middle-class children would have been vaccinated. Even though not always conscientiously or effectively carried out, the compulsory program was effective enough to see the diminution of small pox well before the onset of the twentieth century.[44]

In 1875, there still was no science of pediatrics and the medical profession in general showed little interest in children's diseases.[45] In the face of the medical science's inability to treat virulent childhood illness, the middle-class mother turned to two other sources for help, neither of which were very productive.

She often sought advice from domestic manuals which contained sections on childhood ailments and diseases: how to recognize them and what relief was available for treating the symptoms (since cures were not known). *Ward & Lock's Home Book* was particularly prolific, giving advice on fevers and skin eruptions, convulsions, thrush, cold and coughs, abscesses of the ear, tooth rash, vomiting, whooping cough (the nondangerous kind), headache, diarrhea, ring worm, and croup, among others.[46] The manual also gave advice which complemented whatever medical advice the mother was given regarding measles (deemed contagious but not ordinarily dangerous), chicken-pox (contagious, also not dangerous), and scarlet fever (more dangerous).[47] The same book gave first-aid suggestions for, among other things, wounds, cuts, bruises, and strains, with notes on what a mother's medicine chest should contain.[48]

Another alternative was to go to the chemist and buy a patent medicine whose advertisements promised relief. Unknown to the mother, however, many of the medicines bought over the counter contained opiates; these, when administered to little children whose body systems were too fragile to tolerate them, often resulted in convulsions, a major source of death for very young children throughout the century.[49]

Still, when doctors could not help, mothers simply did what they could. The fact that sometimes the measures they took when their children were ill did more harm than good was simply a commentary on the helplessness of everyone, professionals and laity alike, in the face of bodily infection, a state that lasted well into the twentieth century.

In a different category were the child-health deficiencies which were not life-threatening but of concern to the middle-class mother as the children grew up; for example, the state of her children's teeth and eyesight. Children were taught to brush their teeth, using soda and salt as dentifrices, and in 1892, a prepared product in a tube called Buchan's Tooth Paste appeared on the market.[50] (No statistics have been gathered regarding the incidence of bad teeth among middle-class children, but studies made of the teeth of poor school children at Sutton in Surrey and in central London showed an appalling incidence of tooth decay.)[51]

As far as poor eyesight was concerned, middle-class parents who could afford to send their boys to grammar school found the school provided spectacles where needed. The 1890s "was the decade of the spread of the middle-class children's glasses and the emergence of the bespectacled swot."[52]

No information is available about the provision of dental care or eye glasses for growing girls.

As the middle-class matron and her husband grew older, adult ailments became, if not a preoccupation, something which intruded more and more upon their lives. Illnesses such as dropsy, edema of the legs (associated with ulcerated varicose veins), liver disease, kidney disease, stomach disorders, diarrhea, lung inflammation, and dysentery were all medically noted, if not helped.[53] Heart disease, whose symptoms seem to have been implicitly recognized throughout the century, was a disease for which there was no cure.[54] Another was, of course, cancer, which saw an enormous inexplicable increase among males between 1851 and 1890. Still, because of the high incidence of female breast cancer, cancer in general caused the deaths of 25 percent more women than men at century's end.[55]

By the 1890s, our middle-class married woman was in her forties, her husband even older. While male adult life expectancy had increased from 39.9 years between 1838 and 1854 to 44 by 1890, in the same period, life expectancy for female adults increased from 41.9 in 1838 to 47 in 1890.[56]

During the nineteenth century, middle age became old age at about 45 years.[57] However, concern about the assorted geriatric illnesses for the really old so prevalent in present-day society probably was irrelevant to this couple since neither the middle-class married woman nor her spouse would have lived long enough to have experienced any of them.

NOTES

1. Branca, *Silent Sisterhood*, 62.
2. As is evident from the printed menus, the meal suggestions

and the marketing lists for these years were found in every household domestic manual.
  3. Branca, *Silent Sisterhood*, 70.
  4. Wohl, *Endangered Lives*, 329.
  5. F. B. Smith, *The People's Health, 1830–1910* (New York: Holmes & Meier, 1979), 290, 328.
  6. Mitchell, *Daily Life*, 197.
  7. Branca, *Silent Sisterhood*, 65, 67.
  8. Ibid., 70.
  9. Mitchell, *Daily Life*, 193.
  10. Branca, *Silent Sisterhood*, 86.
  11. Ibid., 86–89.
  12. Ibid., 86.
  13. Smith, *The People's Health*, 13.
  14. Ibid.
  15. Ibid.
  16. Isabella Beeton saw breast-feeding as a definite health hazard for the mother. She observed that "Lactation is always an exhausting process. . . . The nine or twelve months a woman usually suckles must be, to some extent, to most mothers a period of privation and penance." Beeton, *Book of Home Management*, 1034–35; quoted in Branca, *Silent Sisterhood*, 103.
  17. Ibid., 103–4.
  18. Ibid.
  19. Wohl, *Endangered Lives*, 23.
  20. Branca, *Silent Sisterhood*, 103–4.
  21. William Farr, *Vital Statistics* (1885), as quoted in Peter Gay, *Education of the Senses*, vol. 1 of *The Bourgeois Experience: Victoria to Freud* (London: Oxford Press, 1984), 234.
  22. Branca, *Silent Sisterhood*, 96.
  23. Ibid., 98.
  24. Smith, *The People's Health*, 69, 93–94; also Branca, *Silent Sisterhood*, 99.
  25. Branca, *Silent Sisterhood*, 99.
  26. Wohl, *Endangered Lives*, 21–23.
  27. Ibid., 21.
  28. Ibid., 22.
  29. Ibid.
  30. Ibid., 23.

31. Branca, *Silent Sisterhood*, 99.
32. Ibid., 108–9.
33. Ibid., 108.
34. Smith, *The People's Health*, 136.
35. Ibid.
36. Ibid., 139.
37. Ibid.
38. Ibid.
39. Ibid., 151.
40. Ibid., 143.
41. Ibid., 142–43.
42. Mitchell, *Victorian Britain*, 832.
43. Smith, *The People's Health*, 160.
44. Ibid., 170.
45. Branca, *Silent Sisterhood*, 98.
46. *Ward & Lock's Home Book*, 456–96.
47. Ibid., 456–96.
48. Ibid., 489–98.
49. Branca, *Silent Sisterhood*, 106.
50. Smith, *The People's Health*, 180.
51. Ibid., 181.
52. Ibid., 184.
53. Ibid., 323.
54. Ibid., 325.
55. Ibid., 329–30.
56. Ibid., 197.
57. Ibid., 316.

CHAPTER 11

The Matron as Nurturer of the Children: Early Child Care and Education

The new mother's ready assumption of responsibility for the care and early education of her children was based on the unquestioned belief that mothering was innate to her as it was to all women. However, she never presumed she would do the rearing entirely on her own. Sometimes, if her mother or older sisters lived nearby, she sought help from them; but in the main, she turned to the experts who spoke out from the pages of women's magazines and domestic manuals in order to learn the most up-to-date methods of child guidance.

For the middle class of limited income, the mother was the chief caretaker throughout the children's preschool years.[1] This did not mean that she did it without help from the servants; on the contrary, the number of servants involved in caring for children nearly doubled between 1851 and 1881.[2] In fact, by personally taking control of the children's early education, the middle-class mother needed more, not less, help in doing all the work involved.[3]

Women of moderate means did not ordinarily follow the upper-class practice of hiring a children's nurse/educator known as a nanny who, though untrained in a formal sense, was skilled in child care and training, having learned her craft in an apprenticeship system from her own mother or as a nursemaid.[4] (In the wealthier homes, the nanny was actually a mother-substitute, often serving in the household from the birth of the first child until the last child graduated from the nursery to a governess/tutor or preparatory school.)[5]

In the first place, it was too expensive. A family with a yearly income in the low-£300 range could not afford to hire a child nurse who demanded a wage of £25 to £35 per annum.[6] Then, sometimes, middle-class mothers chose not to hire a nanny because, (as explained earlier) they were persuaded of the inadvisability in putting their children in charge of a domestic who might possibly use ungrammatical speech, be prone to drink or disorderly behavior, or not show the proper vigilance in the matter of cleanliness.[7]

In a more positive sense, the new mother did not want a servant as a mother-substitute at all; she wished to devote all her energies to raising the children herself.[8]

Her solution to the problem of the children's care was to hire a nursemaid: a younger, less experienced child care-giver who could be hired for a considerably lower wage than a nanny and who would take over the onerous child-care duties while she, the mother, did the nurturing.[9] The nursemaid's main job was to clean up after the children, feed them, dress them, take them out for walks and watch over them when the mother was otherwise occupied.[10] In the house, she was also delegated the heavy work of tending the nursery fires and carrying the hot water and meals up and down the stairs to and from the nursery.[11] In addition, she sometimes was asked to do housecleaning as well.[12]

As might be expected, the nursemaid often was in complete charge of the children while the mother was busy taking care of other things. Unfortunately, because this domestic was very young and untrained for the job, the care and attention she gave the children was far below the mother's standards and certainly less than what might be expected from an older nanny. While hiring a nursemaid rather than a nanny was unquestionably easier on the family's budget, this child-care alternative did not provide the best care for the Victorian child.[13]

Guidance advice offered to new mothers in the domestic manuals was voluminous. One book carefully instructed the mother on the physical aspects of the nursery: its location (i.e., not too isolated from the parents' quarters—yet not so close as to impinge totally on the mother's privacy) and the proper furniture and furnishings to have in it,[14] the implication being that, if the nursery were well ordered, the child and the mother would be affected in an agreeable way. Others gave detailed instructions on how to wash and dress the children, what clothes they should wear, how to provide good air, exercise and sleep, what and how to feed them, and how to take care of their many ailments,[15] should the mother be unable to manage these matters by herself.

An expanded child-caring role for the mother was part of a change in child-raising concepts that began in mid-century and continued beyond century's end. The new attitude, as expressed in the literature these women read, now saw each child as a unique individual with very particular needs that only a loving mother could fulfill.[16] There was a great deal of discussion, for example, on crying: whether the traditional attitude of insisting that crying was good for the child was as correct as the new, developing opinion that urged mothers to find out why the child cried and then to eliminate or relieve whatever it was that was making the child uncomfortable.[17] Similar discussions ensued on the pros and cons of harsh discipline; and by the third quarter of the century, the principle had evolved that "the mother [should] direct the child positively, through love, kindness, and a soft manner,"[18] with physical punishment used only as a last resort.

It is interesting to note that, while these new modes of child care were supposed to involve both parents, the advice was given primarily (as it would be for years into the future) to the mother.[19] Even if one rejects the image of the autocratic Victorian father as depicted in fiction, fathers apparently played little part in the early training of the children. Possibly the explanation was simple: they weren't around the house while the children were growing up.[20] In fact, anecdotal sources indicate that then, as even now, fathers who did not have responsibility to discipline the children often tended to spoil them, exasperating the mother by showering the children with toys and special privileges.[21]

Very early childhood education started at infancy with the mother playing with the baby in the cradle, singing lullabies at bedtime, reciting nursery rhymes to the child at odd moments, and playing finger games,[22] as common then as they are today. As the babies became toddlers, the mother might retire to the nursery with them during the mornings when she was free, to read them books (there was an ample curriculum of proper children's books at the bookstalls if the mother wanted to avail herself of them), tell them Bible stories or read uplifting poetry, teach them drawing and paper cutting, or give them simple lessons in geography and history.[23]

Considering the other demands on the mother's time and the many chores of the nursemaid, the children probably had a minimum of supervision during their preschool years. In fact, they were expected to amuse themselves or play with each other in the nursery when not actually involved in eating (usually with the family, when they were old enough), sleeping, walking out with the nursemaid, or engaged in family-related functions.[24] Their games were familiar ones middle-class children have always played: blind man's buff, hide and seek, hunt the thimble, charades, and make-believe.[25] Girls played with dolls and doll houses, boys had hobbyhorses, rocking horses, models of ships, lead soldiers, and kites.[26] (Except for this difference in toys, there was little difference in the way boys and girls were treated in the same nursery).[27] Curiosity and imagination were expected to made up for any lack in elaborate toys or instruction.[28]

In some families preschool children were schooled. Formal instruction often began in the nursery long before kindergarten age, although most of this was moral education: teaching them obedience, good manners, respect for their elders and ethical precepts. Whether preschool children in the late 1870s and early 1880s were schooled as rigorously as anecdotal history tells us some children were in early Victorian years is not known,[29] but in the unlikely possibility that this was deemed necessary, the instruction was just for the boys. In such a case, a daily governess or tutor of sorts came in to give lessons in particular subjects, or for certain hours in the day.[30]

Once the boys reached the age of six, however, their education became a matter of serious attention; casual maternal instruction no longer sufficed. In most cases where formal instruction was concerned, the middle-class mother, who herself had no extensive schooling, was often uncertain of her ability to do the job. "Formal education" became the responsibility for "teachers" in a "school"; and once this became evident, the woman's direct role in her sons' educational upbringing began to decline.

Until the first Educational Act was passed in 1870, the education of children was voluntary; the Act created the first national system of compulsory elementary education which at first supplemented and later ultimately replaced the voluntary school system with state-sponsored institutions.[31] However, there is little indication that middle-class parents of limited income sent their children in any appreciable numbers to the state-sponsored Board schools; in fact, anecdotal and self-revelatory literature seems to suggest that these middle-class parents viewed state schools with distaste, seeing them as primarily for working-class children, far too egalitarian for their children.[32]

Given the family income restraints, there were not many

alternatives open to the parents who wanted their children (i.e., their boys) formally educated. Their preference probably was to send the boys to high-fee public schools or to private proprietary establishments. By century's end there were about one hundred public schools with perhaps 30,000 pupils, intended to provide education for the elite.[33]

But the total cost of educating even one son for a profession ran in the order of £1,500 to £2,000, spread over perhaps ten years.[34] When this sum was multiplied by the number of boys in the family, such an expense could become a heavy financial burden for the middle-class family, forcing the parents to consider the less attractive alternatives of sending the boys to grammar schools, which offered secondary schooling beyond the Three Rs, or to one of a variety of independent schools, often housed in private homes that were found in the suburbs.[35]

At this point the education of the boys, a story to be found elsewhere, was the mother's responsibility no longer. Educating the girls, however, continued to come under her jurisdiction—or at least it was an area from which she was not specifically excluded.

Unless she or her girls were particularly attracted at an early age to school outside the home, it is most probable that, for families who were too poor to afford a governess, the mother taught them herself until they were nine or ten,[36] despite misgivings she may have felt regarding her own educational inadequacies.

Beyond that age, there were alternatives. One was to send the girls to a private day school for a few years,[37] or even to the state public day schools.[38] It seems unlikely that the girls' parents would copy what was done in some more pretentious middle-class families by sending their girls to those small boarding schools that drilled them in the "accomplishments" (that is, talents such as piano playing, embroidery, perhaps a smattering of French, and water-color painting) and fed them an array of facts, usually taught parrot-wise.[39] Since the average cost of a reasonably good private boarding school education for girls was a high £130 a year (although there were some poor-quality schools for less),[40] it seems reasonable to assume that an expensive secondary education for the girls was not a matter of high priority.[41]

To employ a governess full time over a long period to educate the girls was generally too expensive for this family; meager as the £30 per annum salary of a governess seemed to be, it was a high annual outlay to undertake for any length of time.[42] In the city, the middle-class families often used an intermittent combination of home education, daily governesses for short periods, and day schools until their daughters were into their teens.[43]

In the 1870s and for succeeding decades, a new type of middle-class girls' school established in London and provincial cities proved particularly successful. These were the Girls Public Day School Company and High Schools, with curricula modeled after boys' schools (Latin, sometimes Greek, math, history, and the sciences) and with classwork very goal-organized.[44] Designed to emulate a public institution, they avoided as much as possible the model of earlier girls' schools that sought to copy a home environment. Although fees were charged, they were quite reasonable and the schools provided girls with a surprisingly good education.[45]

By the end of the century, a change of attitude regarding the formal training of girls to do paid work before marriage took place, as reflected in articles published in the domestic magazines[46]—and this new outlook was adopted by many middle-class mothers, even those who were not particularly "advanced" in their views. Though it was still held that paid work did not further the femininity of the woman, training for the newly opened employment opportunities in the civil service and commercial offices was now regarded as a useful, even a necessary, experience for the middle-class girl.[47] By the last decade of the century, sending daughters to school to be trained as "type-writers" (women who used machines rather than pens to write) was an educational possibility that middle-class mothers grew to accept with equanimity.[48]

Some experts, in fact, suggested that training girls for employment in the higher professions such as nursing or school teaching, not just temporary clerking jobs, was not only good as an educational experience but increased her chances for matrimony, because "the workplace provided many possibilities for meeting men."[49] However, this was not a universal sentiment. In the eyes of the middle-class mother, girls who had achieved an early education of sorts and possibly some training in the business world had no further need for higher education. A girl's future occupation was expected to be the same as her mother's: that of being a married woman.[50]

NOTES

1. Gorham, *The Feminine Ideal*, 17.
2. McBride, " 'As the Twig Is Bent,' " 47.
3. Ibid., 48.
4. Ibid., 50–51.
5. Mitchell, *Victorian Britain*, 551.
6. Beeton, *Book of Household Management*, 16.
7. Turner, *What the Butler Saw*, 144.
8. McBride, " 'As the Twig Is Bent,' " 48.
9. Ibid., 46.
10. Ibid., 51.
11. Mitchell, *Victorian Britain*, 551.
12. McBride, " 'As the Twig Is Bent,' " 48–49.
13. Ibid., 49.
14. Panton, *From Kitchen to Garrett*, 160–76.
15. *Spons' Household Manual*, 746–53.
16. Branca, *Silent Sisterhood*, 108–9.
17. Ibid., 109.
18. Ibid., 110.
19. Ibid., 111.
20. Ibid., 110.
21. Beryl Lee Booker, *Yesterday's Child, 1890–1909* (London: John Long, 1937), 221–22.

22. In *The Pre-School Age: A Mother's Guide to a Child's Occupation* (a guide not only to unorganized preschooling training but to organized teaching, addressed specifically to an American audience), Minnie Watson-Kamm proposed a variety of activities for the preschooler, including these suggestions.
23. Ibid.
24. Panton, *From Kitchen to Garrett*, 179.
25. Christopher Hibbert, *The Horizon Book of Daily Life in Victorian England* (New York: American Heritage Publishers, 1975), 35.
26. Ibid., 45–46.
27. Gorham, *The Feminine Ideal*, 17–18.
28. Panton, *From Kitchen to Garrett*, 178–79.
29. Mitchell, *Victorian Britain*, 41. John Stuart Mill's father, for example, began teaching him Greek and Latin at age three; while Matthew Arnold learned French, Latin grammar, math, history, and geography at age five, then Greek, German, and Italian the following year.
30. Mitchell, *Daily Life*, 178.
31. J.F.C. Harrison, *Late Victorian Britain, 1870–1901* (Glasgow: Fontana, 1990), 200.
32. Ibid.
33. Ibid., 203.
34. Thompson, *Respectable Society*, 66.
35. J.F.C. Harrison, *Late Victorian Britain*, 203.
36. Mitchell, *Daily Life*, 181.
37. Ibid.
38. Ibid., 180–181.
39. Avery, *Victorian People*, 122–23.
40. Joan Perkin, *Victorian Women* (London: John Murray, 1993), 32.
41. Thompson, *Respectable Society*, 66.
42. Gorham, *The Feminine Ideal*, 20.
43. Mitchell, *Daily Life*, 181.
44. Gorham, *The Feminine Ideal*, 25.
45. Ibid., 26.
46. Margaret Beetham, *A Magazine of Her Own? Domesticity and Desire in the Woman's Magazine, 1800–1914* (London: Routledge, 1996), 141.

47. Ibid.
48. Gorham, *The Feminine Ideal*, 116–17.
49. From an article by a Mrs. Elser, " 'Between Ourselves': A Friendly Chat with the Girls," in *The Young Woman* 4 (1895–96), as quoted by Gorham, *The Feminine Ideal*, 117.
50. Ibid., 120.

CHAPTER 12

The Matron as Social Secretary and Activities Coordinator

The stay-at-home matron expedited all the social functions within the family, acting as organizer, often instigator, director, and cleaner-upper, much the same then as fifty years later. It was her job to arrange things, plan ahead, and take care of contingencies. This recitation of what the *family* did all day shows the matron always involved behind the scenes, a very low-profile agent-in-charge.

Most of her early obligations involved the children: she arranged home entertainments, informal dinners, and parties for them. She sometimes took them on outings to the city, sometimes to visit the zoo or Madame Tussaud's waxworks; at other times to the local suburban fairs that offered sideshow exhibitions as at a carnival.[1] At home, she frequently acted as inn-keeper/hostess for friends of the children who came as "vacation visitors," to stay for a few days, perhaps longer. Later in time, as her daughters grew older, she took them window shopping on Oxford and Regent streets, to gaze at the exotic foods on display at Fortnum & Mason or to browse through Harrods.[2] After the children passed through adolescence and became young adults interested in more grown-up socializing, she arranged picnics, bicycle outings, musicals at home, or informal dances for them.

One of her duties, as might be expected, was to be co-ordinator of all family activities. Sometimes she acted for the nuclear family alone, at other times managed reunions for the broader family, both her own and her husband's. Gathering for Christmas, was one such reunion, often celebrated as a tradition in the middle-class Christian family.

In anticipation of the Christmas festivities, the housewife was, of course, involved with the food preparation and meal planning, seeing that various bedrooms were cleaned and made ready (if there were outside guests staying at the home) and, once the frivolities began, making sure that cleaning up and dish-washing was done on a continuous basis.

The celebration usually began with shopping for Christmas cards (an innovation introduced in mid-century), done by both parents and children; and the buying—and hiding—of gifts for the rest of the family was one in which the matron was very much involved. Next, the Christmas tree (a German custom brought to England by Prince Albert) was put up and decorated with toys, ribbons, fancy papers, and candles.[3] Later she saw to it that a special Christmas Eve dinner for friends and family was served, followed by the opening of gifts, carol singing, and the presentation of pantomimes and home theatricals.[4] On Christmas morning, after the children had taken down their Christmas stockings tacked to the fireplace mantle, she and the family went to church, and following church, she took part in organized, ritualized gestures of charity such as taking food to a poor family.[5]

The day after Christmas Day, known as Boxing Day, was the servants' holiday and often the occasion for more parties. On Boxing Day, one family activity was often a visit to the pantomimes (musical revues with elaborate production numbers enjoyed by virtually every social class), which began on the day after Christmas.[6]

A different but analagous family activity occurring approximately six months after the Christmas festivities was the Summer Holiday at the Seashore for the nuclear family alone (and often one servant), an indulgence practiced by all income strata within the middle class.[7] For the housewife, this was even more strenuous that hosting the Christmas celebration.

Every year the family would rent rooms at a boarding house in a resort town on the ocean for a fortnight.[8] Places like Brighton, Tunbridge Wells, or Scarborough, earlier the playgrounds of the aristocracy and gentry, had been taken over in mid-century by a solid middle-class clientele, and resorts at places such as Bournemouth, Eastbourne, Folkstone, and Hove were especially developed to meet the middle-class demand.[9]

Sometimes, if the man or his wife knew a family with similar tastes, the two families would rent a house for an entire month together; in that event the men commuted to the city during the week and came out on weekends, while the children and women vacationed on the beach.[10] Despite recurring discussions about "where to go this year," the family usually returned to the same place, year after year.[11]

To arrange the Summer Holiday took careful initial planning by the housewife; after that it was just a matter of doing or delegating the work to be done.

The first-time decision of where to go was the most time-consuming. The housewife canvassed all their friends and relatives for names of a good resort area with a pleasure pier or promenade, with a sandy sea front and rows of bathing machines, with a bandstand and pantomimes.[12] Most important, she looked for a boarding house where people of the same social status as they stayed. For the names and descriptions of the various rentals available, she consulted guidebooks, wrote away for free brochures giving comparative rates, and looked in the newspaper for summer vacancy advertisements.[13]

Going off to the resort was an involved undertaking; preparations began weeks in advance.[14] Wardrobes had to be checked and rechecked, new clothes bought (informal but not too informal),[15] trunks pulled out of storage places, and clothing packed.[16] (However, a review of the summer clothes—what to take, what to put aside as no longer serviceable, what new to buy—was part of a seasonal clothing checklist that had to be done whether the family went away from the city or not.)

It was a time of exciting anticipation for the children but hardly that for the housewife. She did the packing with the help of a servant, trying to remember what had to be taken along in case of unexpected contingencies as well as making sure everything would be done properly at home in the family's absence, including delegating what the rest of the servants were to do.

On the day of departure, a hired van was loaded with all the bags and baggage, and the family (with at least one servant) was taken to the rail terminal. They went by train, travelling second class.[17] At their destination all the boxes and trunks were transferred to another van and taken to the boarding house where they settled into their rooms to start the holiday.

At least the husband and the children settled in. The woman and the general servant first arranged for the unpacking: drawers were lined with paper, clothes put away, toys sorted out, and the trunks removed to wherever they would be kept until repacking time. Then the mistress settled affairs with the proprietor: finding out where the servant was to sleep and eat, arranging for such things as beach chairs for the adults and sand pails and shovels for the children, learning about eating times, checking on picnic possibilities or where she could find a washerwoman if necessary, and so forth. Then she settled in.

While mama and papa sat on the beach on deck chairs, the children played and visited and explored (ostensibly under the supervision of the servant).[18] Not much actual swimming was done nor was it really a popular sports activity; since bathing in the ocean was a complicated affair involving the use of a bathing machine (a kind of caravan wagon on wheels, dragged into the sea by a horse, in which people undressed and dressed) and, for the women and girls, the wearing of heavy, very full bathing costumes.[19]

But the children played on the beach, went for country walks, took donkey rides, watched the minstrels and Punch and Judy shows on the promenade, listened to the band in the bandstand, and bought candy from round slot machines.[20] The older children went boating and sailing and were permitted to meet other young people with comparatively little restraint.[21]

At the end of the holiday, all the activity of the packing and travelling was repeated in reverse, and the family came home. There everyone relaxed at last, except the woman of the house, of course. Once home, the housewife and the servant unpacked the clothing, assembled those that had to be washed or cleaned or repaired, put away the trunks, planned the evening meal with the cook—or the mistress prepared the food for the family herself. Then she relaxed, home from the country holiday.

As the children grew older, organizing their social activities grew less frequent and those involving her husband's colleagues or the couple's personal friends took up more of the matron's time. (By this time, household tasks had become routine and more readily delegated and the possibility of a more indulgent life seemed less frivolous than in earlier years.)

Social functions, no matter what they were, continued to be evaluated in terms of cost; money remained a problem for the MCMW and the family. Never would this couple ever have enough money so that they could indulge in pleasures without thinking about cost, particularly if these pleasures had no attendant educational or cultural justification. Still, throughout the years, "making do" had become the family lifestyle and the mistress's natural behavior; she could no more be extravagant than she could be slovenly. In this context, she and her husband lived, and entertained, and played, and enjoyed themselves.

A large part of the obligations the matron assumed related specifically to her husband and his work. Among them were probably such organizational tasks as keeping track of social commitments, setting up and running dinner parties for important people, arranging gatherings for colleagues and their wives, and providing the home atmosphere when he entertained men who were important business connections—although never articulated so explicitly.

The entertainment of her husband's colleagues (and their spouses) usually took place in the home where it could be carried on with style without extravagance; these included dinner parties, card parties, musical evenings, and, sometimes, even dances.

Dinner parties were formal affairs, with printed invitations and formal acceptances, wine and foods in vast array, the table set as an elegant display.[22] However, the portrayals of The Dinner Party found in many household manuals, while ostensibly directed to the middle-class, must be seen more correctly as examples of elegant living undertaken only by the wealthy middle-class and the upper-classes (even royalty). In Mrs. Beeton's book, for example, a description of a specimen dinner party detailed the extravagant table setting, the food prepared and served (she printed a menu, in English and in French, of an eight-course meal of soup, fish, entrees, remove, roast, sweets, savoury, and dessert), the manner of service, the behavior, demeanor, and roles of the many servants, the kind of conversation allowed or not allowed, with exact descriptions of the rituals of entrance, seating, and departure.[23] This most certainly could not have been the kind of formal dinner party this middle-class woman prepared for her guests.

The party organized by the middle-class matron did follow a set ritual, but its format was tempered by economy, expediency, and perhaps a distaste for excessive formality.[24] (On the other hand, since elaborate dinner parties were not given often, on their occasion the hostess may have indulged in somewhat more formality and style than ordinary entertaining required.)

Invitations were sent out about two weeks before the event. Dinner was set for 7:30 or 8:30 P.M., and guests were expected to arrive punctually. Everyone gathered in the upstairs drawing room (or some room other than the dining room), but no drinks were served. When all had arrived and dinner was ready, they then proceeded to the dining room as mixed couples (the men and women intentionally paired so as to encourage lively conversation) and sat in designated places at the table, which was bedecked with flowers.

If the hostess was serving the dinner in the fashionable "Russian-style," she would have hired extra help, since in order to serve it servants were constantly removing food from the sideboard and circling the table, offering food to the guests continuously, not as courses, changing plates and silverware as the food was eaten. (Mrs. Beeton did warn, in one of her book's many editions, that serving dinner *à la russe* was not really suitable for a small gathering.)[25] Otherwise, the dinner was served *à la française*, a more relaxing service that came one course at a time.

The dinner might include a choice of soup; a choice of fish; entrees of beef, chicken, or sweetbreads; another course of veal, lamb, roast fowl, or ham with cooked vegetables of many kinds; still another course of various fowl, condiments, and vegetables; and then desserts, fruits of the season, and ices.

After dinner, the women left for the drawing room for coffee or tea while the men remained at the table with their port or brandy and cigarettes. Eventually they joined the women in the drawing room for coffee and tea, and still more pleasant conversation, sometimes followed by cards or a little music. Ordinarily, after these pleasantries, the guests were expected to leave promptly; they were generally gone by eleven o'clock.[26]

Other evening functions were less formal and much more

fun, such as the Musical Evening, whose purpose was more for the social intermingling than the quality of the music.[27] This involved complete audience participation, with some individuals rising to sing ballads or patriotic songs, others being cajoled to render favorite songs about home or the plight of the orphan, or men reciting stirring poetry (Tennyson and Kipling being two favorites).[28] Everyone eventually went home with a lot of chatter and laughter, the evening pronounced a huge success.

Some functions were "couple" affairs outside the home which the matron, often in conjunction with the other women in their group, arranged. Going to the theatre was one such activity.

The middle class was a great supporter of the theatre (unless, of course, their religion forbade it).[29] If they lived in the suburbs, they did not ordinarily go to the West End; instead, they supported their local suburban theatres and the actor-managers who ran them, who, in turn, catered almost on a personal basis to the tastes of their middle-class patrons.[30] For these people, going to the theatre was a year-round activity, not reserved for the few weeks of the "Season" as Society saw it.[31] By the last quarter of the century, theatres and concerts were accepted activities that even the middle-class religious sects indulged in; those who were adamant on the wickedness of plays attended performances of oratorios (sacred music being allowed) and orchestral concerts when viewed as "cultural events" rather than just amusement.[32]

When the man and his wife attended the theatre with their friends, they did not go in formal clothes, but they did wear their best suit and frock. Their seats were in the Pit or the Gallery—or even the Upper Circle, where places could be reserved.[33] The cost of an entire evening of enjoyment was very reasonable: only 2s. 6d. a seat, no tax, in the Pit.[34] It was said, perhaps in jest, that getting tickets for the theatre was the only thing the middle-class would queue up for.[35]

Sometimes the man and his wife went to dinner in the city

with friends. By the last quarter of the century, excellent restaurants, all of which by then welcomed women, were to be found throughout the West End, the names of the most worthy (both in style and in moderate prices) being well known in their circles. They could dine in style at the Holborn Restaurant, for example, and enjoy six courses, with music, for only 2s. 6d. per person.[36] Or, if they preferred, they could go to one of the many American-style grand hotels which, by the 1880s, had opened their dining rooms to nonresidents and were offering meals at reasonable prices.[37]

Music-halls, being essentially male-oriented and somewhat indelicate and even vulgar (but rarely "blue"), were not ordinarily the entertainment of choice of the middle class. Women seldom went there in the more uninhibited days of music hall popularity in mid-century, even if accompanied, although they did later in the century when the music-halls themselves become more respectable.[38]

At the very end of the century, another social entertainment appeared, the motion picture. It was called the kinetoscope or cinematograph at the Empire theatre when it opened in March, 1896, and the anamatograph at the Alhambra theatre, which opened at about the same time.[39] Sometimes, in an adventurous mood, the couple would visit the show houses just to see what it was like, but, in general, going to the motion pictures was not the preferred entertainment of the middle class.[40]

As the matron and her husband grew older, the woman began to plan activities just for the two of them, such as taking a Cook's group holiday to Wales or Scotland.[41] But the high point of this couple's social aspirations, the great recreational occasion of their lives, came in their older years when they took a holiday abroad with the Thomas Cook travel agency. It was probably done only once during the marriage, and the trip was relived over and over in retelling and discussion with friends.

In mid-century, the Thomas Cook travel agency began arranging middle-class tours, with middle-class fares, to France, Switzerland, and Italy; by the 1880s even trips to see the pyramids of Egypt were possible (Cook had invested both in Egyptian hotels and river steamers to insure safety and comfort for the English tourists).[42] Some trips, such as a cruise of the Nile for a couple, were very expensive, £200–£300, and possibly out of reach financially for this particular middle-class couple; but a six-week package tour for two to the Rhine, Switzerland, and France, cost only £85[43] and might be undertaken as a once-in-a-lifetime trip. On such a tour, the couple would indulge in all the cultural activities they had up to then never before enjoyed: visiting art galleries and churches, studying architecture and antiquities, going to the opera and musical affairs, even mountaineering while in Switzerland.[44] In time, Cook even sponsored an abbreviated and edited version of the upper-class's Grand Tour of Europe, offering the middle-class who traveled in groups throughout Europe special cut-rate railway prices.[45] When such a trip was planned, involving as it did meetings with the agent in the city and the transfer of much money, the husband probably made the arrangements rather than the housewife.

In some of these travel activities, particularly when they were not all-inclusive, arranged affairs, the matron often had less of a vacation than the others in the party. While she frequently had experiences involving exotic places she never would not otherwise have visited, often she also carried on the same functions that she did at home: packing up, cleaning after, arranging things, and putting away, only at more inconvenient locations. For many years, she worked while the others played—and not until late in her marriage did she realize that she too could become an active participant in the social functions instead of being simply the domestic expeditor.

NOTES

1. Hibbert, *The Horizon Book*, 38.
2. Ibid.
3. Gloag, *Victorian Comfort*, 178.
4. Mitchell, *Victorian Britain*, 153
5. Mitchell, *Daily Life*, 211.
6. Ibid., 213.
7. Macqueen-Pope, *Twenty Shillings*, 97.
8. Ibid., 97.
9. Thompson, *Respectable Society*, 256.
10. Macqueen-Pope, *Twenty Shillings*, 97.
11. Ibid., 98–99.
12. Gloag, *Victorian Comfort*, 174.
13. Macqueen-Pope, *Twenty Shillings*, 99.
14. Ibid.
15. Ibid., 100.
16. Ibid., 102–3.
17. Ibid., 103.
18. Ibid.
19. Ibid., 104–6.
20. Ibid., 107–8.
21. Ibid., 109.
22. Ibid., 251–55; also Marion Lochhead, *The Victorian Household* (London: John Murray, 1964), 38.
23. Beeton, *Book of Household Management*, 21–26, 1682–91, 1693–94. Although descriptions in Mrs. Beeton's book changed over the years, becoming gradually less upper-class oriented with each successive edition, the difference was primarily a matter of degree. The 1909 edition, for example, included the menu of a banquet served to His Majesty, King George III.
24. What follows is an amalgamation and extrapolation of descriptions in Mitchell, *Daily Life*, 127–29; Marion Lochhead, *The Victorian Household*, 38–41; Macqueen-Pope, *Twenty Shillings*, 251–54; and Daniel Pool, *What Jane Austin Ate and Charles Dickens Knew, from Hunting to Whist: The Facts of Daily Life in Nineteenth-Century England* (New York: Simon & Schuster, 1993), 72–77.

25. Robertson, *History of the Housewife*, 34.
26. Macqueen-Pope, *Twenty Shillings*, 255.
27. Ibid., 256.
28. Ibid., 256–63.
29. Ibid., 264.
30. Ibid.
31. Ibid., 265.
32. Thompson, *Respectable Society*, 255.
33. Macqueen-Pope, *Twenty Shillings*, 265.
34. Ibid., 266.
35. Ibid., 267.
36. Metcalf, *Victorian London*, 150.
37. Mitchell, *Victorian Britain*, 667.
38. Macqueen-Pope, *Twenty Shillings*, 273.
39. Metcalf, *Victorian Britain*, 169.
40. Macqueen-Pope, *Twenty Shillings*, 276.
41. Thompson, *Respectable Society*, 261.
42. Ibid., 262.
43. Ibid., 262–63.
44. Ibid., 263.
45. Ibid., 264.

CHAPTER 13

The Matron as Morals Arbiter: Managing the Family's Religious and Charitable Obligations

For middle-class Christian families, the time-honored Victorian custom, from the 1830s well into the 1870s, of holding family prayers just before breakfast for everyone (children, servants, adults, and visitors alike), was gradually being replaced in the century's last quarter by a Sunday evening gathering in the home. Soon even this would be abandoned altogether by century's end.[1] But what replaced it and what role the middle-class married woman played in the religious practices of the family at home is not clear. The amount of research done in this area, focusing on late- rather than mid-century and particularly directed to this income stratum, has been sparse, with no attention at all given to the activities of the stay-at-home mistress of the house.

According to Charles Booth, who researched the lives of the people of London at the end of the nineteenth century, religious patterns of the lower middle class as a whole varied from district to district, with no established norm of church-going habits to be found among them.[2] One recent researcher found that, as a group, the lower middle class was more nonconformist in religious observances than those in the higher income brackets although not necessarily antagonistic to the church, particularly since they were under no pressure, as their "betters" were, to set a standard for a household of servants.[3]

As a corollary to the decline in religious commitment, this period of time saw a gradual disappearance of "the Victorian Sabbath," with its extended list of prohibited activities intruding on the solemnity of Sunday. An organization called the National Sunday League formed with the expressed purpose of opening up Sunday as a day of recreation (provided that, as they made clear, the Sunday recreation flowed into "healthy channels").[4] While the group agitated strongly for the Sunday opening of museum and art galleries, this relaxation did not come about until 1896.[5]

What religious authority was exercised inside the family circle by both parents appeared to be minimal: the mother told Bible stories and taught the children to say their prayers, and both the mother and the father passed on to them moral standards of behavior that reflected the conscientious, work-oriented values of the middle-class.[6] While ethical in content, this last was not religious teaching in a true sense.

In general the middle-class families in this group gravitated to their neighborhood religious center less as a gesture of piety than to meet like-minded friends or to make new ones, though the degree of religious commitment among the church members varied a great deal and regular church attendance appeared to be relatively low.[7] The renting of a family pew and attendance at services was less a gesture of religious commitment than an expression of their pleasure in associating with respectable sections of the community like themselves.[8]

For the family, the outside place of worship became the focus of its social life as well. In addition to providing sermons and Sunday school for the children, it served as the center of a network of local clubs and associations for its members, offering activities such as dances, socials, discussions, and amateur theatricals for the family's participation and enjoyment.[9]

But the ritual of observing Sunday by attending church services continued to be ubiquitous in England through to the last decades, long after the custom of religious indoctrination had passed from the family repertoire. The adults attended Sunday services for its main attraction, one that held enormous appeal: listening to the sermon.[10] In large part, the Sunday sermon had become an element contributing to a growing awareness by the congregants of the world and issues of import, an interest that had a resurgence among the middle class in the century's last decades.[11] Ministers among the Unitarians, Congregationalists and Presbyterians, and even some Methodist and Anglican churchmen, were expected to keep abreast of currents in modern culture, discuss controversial books of the day, and debate matters that the congregation felt it should be informed about.[12] The stimulus of the minister's sermon gave many of these nondoctrinnaire churchgoers a context of pragmatic, moral, of-this-world religion that they found congenial.[13]

On the other hand, middle-class parishioners made it clear they didn't want *too* much controversy. Ministers who were too outspoken became the subject of protests, sometimes even dismissal; congregants didn't mind being preached at as long as the minister did not get overzealous in his preaching.[14]

The middle-class married woman experienced not only a diminution of her religious role in the home but in the influence of religion in her personal life,[15] although she was brought up in a home where religion was a constant. No documentation written by these women has been found to confirm this, but one sees this predilection reflected in the content of the magazines she read. These periodicals became increasingly secular, almost completely lacking in religious content.[16] The *Englishwoman's Domestic Magazine*, for one, stated explicitly that their policy was to exclude all religious compositions and to refuse to answer any theological questions or to publish religious poetry.[17] Such indifference, almost hostility, to religious questions was duplicated among the hundreds of women's magazines circulating on the market.[18]

Still, with no direct evidence one way or the other, it may be that religious practices in the home and the family attitudes towards the church were more traditional and ubiquitous than the magazines seemed to indicate. It is possible that those of the middle class living in the suburbs who made a comfortable income, such as civil servants or small-business managers (and one does not know if this category now included the MCMW's husband whose income possibly had risen), held more vigorous religious views, even though the less affluent did not.[19] If the man of the house was now, perhaps, an employer with strong ties to the community, he not only participated in the public affairs of the community but was active in his community church, which he probably viewed as the bastion of respectable thought and conservative theology.[20] Still, even if this was so, there are no data to show whether this was reflected in greater religious observance in the man's home or in the religious activities of his wife.

The association of works of charity with religion had been a characteristic of mid-Victorian England, and this may have continued into the later decades of the century, although whether the middle-class housewife used the suburban church as a vehicle for doing good works and dispensing charity is not clear.

There has been a great deal written about the extensive philanthropic endeavors undertaken by upper-class and wealthier middle-class women at the latter part the nineteenth century. In fact, in the 1880s, according to one observer, "doing good became positively fashionable,"[21] with princesses, prime ministers' wives, and celebrated ladies conspicuously in the forefront. The affinity for organized charitable work by the rich and famous, according to this observer, resulted in a virtual "craze for slumming" through the formation of an immense variety of societies aimed at the moral and physical betterment of the poor.[22]

But in the closing decades of the nineteenth century, the ranks of philanthropic organizations more and more became filled with women from the broader middle class. Many were women who had no particular quarrel with their home roles but found such philanthropic work as a way to extend their social horizons.[23] They saw, and persuaded others to see, that charitable work was an extension of domesticity and, through this rationale, were welcomed into the field of social uplift as active volunteer social workers.[24]

The majority of them volunteered for helping services such as tending to the sick and children in institutions or visiting the homes of the poor.[25] While some women saw their volunteer work as a diversion from housework, the most common motivation among middle-class housewives was to extend their domestic roles of caring and sympathy into the community through purposeful work, all the more pleasurable because it was so socially acceptable.[26]

In one sense, the context for philanthropic good works in these later years had become quite different. Earlier in the century, charitable good works were undertaken by women as an end in itself, that is, either as a step toward more important work in the organization or as fulfilling a dedicated mission for personal reasons.[27] By the late nineteenth century, however, philanthropic work was seen as being so much a part of the outward reach of domestic life that organizations became almost exclusively peopled by married women, all serving in a voluntary capacity while continuing full-time duties as housewives.[28]

In the late Victorian period, charitable work proliferated, particularly in the cities, and different groups were formed on behalf of a variety of worthy causes. These projects included such activities as establishing animal shelters, putting up public drinking fountains for horses, establishing libraries and training schools, helping in soup kitchens, working in isolation hospitals, setting up residential homes for the blind, assisting in reformatories[29]—and many many more.

Possibly the middle-class housewife of our study was active in these or other philanthropic endeavors. However, she would not have aggressively and independently sought out a volunteer project of good works to occupy her time. Though she may have sometimes been discontent with the restrictions of her domestic role, there is no indication that she found her stay-at-home life overly restricting and in need of outside stimulation.

It appears more probable that, as far as organized charity was concerned, our matron was a participant but as one of the group, a follower to someone else's call, a willing recruit if someone in her church or chapel or social circle asked her to participate in a worthwhile cause (as, perhaps, wrapping bandages for the sick and wounded in the Boer War or collecting money for a hospital in which the group had an interest). If she was persuaded to do this outside volunteer work, it was always as subsidiary, not in counteraction, to her home responsibilities.

In fact, with the easing of her responsibilities towards others in her home, she possibly was less interested in finding new outside responsibilities than she was—hedonistic as it may sound—in finding ways to indulge in pleasures for herself, as will be detailed subsequently.

NOTES

1. Davidoff, *The Best Circles*, 35–36.
2. See Hugh McLeod, "White Collar Values and the Role of Religion," in *The Lower Middle Class in Britain, 1870–1914*, Geoffrey Crossick, ed. (New York: St. Martin's Press, 1977), 65.
3. Ibid., 66.
4. Ensor, *England, 1870–1914*, 309.
5. Ibid.

6. McLeod, "White Collar Values," 76.
7. Ibid., 72.
8. Ibid., 72–73.
9. Ibid., 73.
10. Hugh McLeod, *Class and Religion in the Late Victorian City* (London: Croom Helm, 1974), 140.
11. Ibid.
12. Ibid., 138.
13. Ibid., 140.
14. Ibid., 143.
15. Branca, *Silent Sisterhood*, 146.
16. Ibid., 147.
17. Ibid.
18. Ibid.
19. McLeod, *Class and Religion*, 148.
20. Ibid., 149–50.
21. Bott and Clephane, *Our Mothers*, 173.
22. Ibid., 174.
23. Jane Lewis, *Women in England, 1870–1950: Sexual Divisions and Social Change* (Brighton, U.K.: Wheatsheaf Books, 1984), 76.
24. Ibid.
25. Ibid., 92.
26. Ibid.
27. Ibid., 95.
28. Ibid.
29. Mitchell, *Daily Life*, 253.

CHAPTER 14

The Matron as Her Own Person: Satisfying Personal Needs Within and Outside the Home

In the first edition of her *Book of Household Management*, Mrs. Beeton advised her readers that "to be a good housewife does not necessarily imply an abandonment of proper leisures or amusing recreation; and we think it the more necessary to express this, as the performance of the duties of a mistress may, to some minds, perhaps seem to be incompatible with the enjoyment of life."[1]

Despite such assurances by this doyen of domestic science that activities of personal fulfillment were not incompatible with family responsibilities, our middle-class mistress of the house remained for many years totally and exclusively devoted to her home and family. When she married in 1875, she fervently believed that her role was to be thoroughly dedicated to her husband, her home and, later, her children, with no selfish thoughts of the need for or the desirability of a life of her own. In fact, so great was her committment to the role as mistress of the home that only the most broadminded of women could have resisted the temptation to turn her back completely on her unmarried friends who still pursued frivolous activities of self-fulfillment; she now favored the company of those who, like herself, were part of a greater, self-sacrificing sorority.

In the early years of her marriage, if she engaged at all in leisure activities of her own, it probably was for very brief intervals, visiting her parents or siblings and only when these visits did not impinge on her home responsibilities.[2] It was only after years of marriage, when housekeeping and mothering duties finally became routine, that she gave any thought to her own needs and pleasures, of reaching out to the life she had left behind.

At such a time, she cautiously began to reconstruct a life of her own, thinking either of doing solitary things that gave her personal pleasure or of socializing with old friends who no longer lived nearby, many of whom were married but some of whom were not. It was a new experience to begin thinking of herself as a person, separate and apart from husband and children.

So what did she do with her newly acquired free time?

Possibly, she chose to stretch out on a chaise in the drawing room and read. The housewife certainly enjoyed reading magazines, particularly those that gave advice on managing a house-enclosed life. In the 1880s and 1890s, many magazines were published that dealt with home topics of interest to housewives, with names like *The Housewife* (1886), *The Mother's Companion* (1887), *The Ladies Home Journal* (1893), and *Woman at Home* (1893)[3] filled with practical information on health, law, fashion, housekeeping, cooking, personal grooming, home furnishings, and dressmaking.[4] These magazines were easy to obtain since her husband could pick them up for her at the railway bookstalls at one or two pence a copy. In addition, on occasion, the magazines even ran articles about the New Women and their ideas (although not necessarily endorsing their views),[5] which she found interesting, though not particularly compelling.

Reading books was another matter. Purchasing books was

comparatively expensive since a universal practice of publishers that continued into the nineties was to publish novels in three volumes at 10s. 6d each, so that buying the entire book cost 31s. 6d. (The "three-decker novels" finally disappeared near the end of the century when they were banned from the shelves of both Mudie's and W. H. Smith in 1894.)[6] While in the later decades cheap editions of books could be bought at one shilling or less,[7] the housewife probably regarded these as working-class editions and would not have chosen them unless she were a very dedicated book reader. Another alternative, that of purchasing in weekly installments those magazines in which a current fast-selling novel was being serialized (that is, having them purchased for her), would have appealed to her only if she were deeply interested in that particular novel.

Borrowing books from a lending library was another option. There were at this time few free public libraries in London to which she had easy access. In fact, the Free Public Library and Reading Room on Smith Street in Westminster was the only free library in London in 1880 from which books could be borrowed and taken away.[8] If she were interested in serious literature or nonfiction, books could be borrowed from two private London libraries, the Times Library and the London Library, but to do so was relatively expensive since each charged a yearly subscription of two guineas.[9]

She would have been much more likely to have turned to the two well-known lending libraries that carried popular titles: Mudie's bookstore—whose lending-library stock consisted mostly of novels but included books on history and biography, travel and adventure—and W. H. Smith, whose bookstalls were to be found in the railway stations and whose circulating library catered to broad, middle-class tastes.[10] Each required a yearly subscription of only one guinea.[11] In order to get books through them, the housewife either had to go to town to borrow or return the books, or ask her husband to do it for her. Still, this might have attracted her if she had joined one of the reading clubs that were becoming fashionable by the last decades of the century—and if she liked to read or had friends who were so inclined.[12]

However, it is debatable whether reading magazines or books at home would have been the housewife's recreation of choice. Being regularly confined to the house, it seems likely that, given free time to spend as she chose, she engaged in an activity that would get her out of the house rather one that kept her indoors as before.

If she went out, it is possible that she did not use her free time for personal pleasure at all, as was explained in the previous chapter; she may have committed herself to doing voluntary social service and charitable good works that had become fashionable. If her friends were doing the same thing at the same time and place, she may have found deep pleasure in the personal companionship as well as the social committment of this work.

Of course, there was always the joys of grandmothering, of visiting her London-based children with families. However, unless her children had been born shortly after she married or unless they married very young, it is not likely that the children would be married with children of their own in the 1890s.

Otherwise, if the matron wanted to spend her time visiting, she may simply have gone to see friends. To see those in her own neighborhood, she walked; otherwise she may have used, in an adventurous and daring mood, a new and comparatively safe (if relatively expensive) foot-propelled mode of transportation called the tricycle,[13] with two large back wheels and a small one in front, comfortable to sit on and easy to steer, wide enough to accommodate her regular clothing.

Unless she was particularly athletic or free-spirited, it is doubtful that she would have chosen a bicycle, which, in any event, was not improved enough to be practicable until the late 1880s. To ride one involved both skill in balancing and sometimes special clothing. The bicycle with equal-sized wheels and a rear-chain drive had been introduced by H. J. Lawson of Brighton in 1874,[14] but it did not achieve popularity until the 1890s when it was improved upon by J. K. Starley (whose Rover model came on the market in 1885)[15] and was equipped with pneumatic tires invented by J. D. Dunlop in 1888.[16] The bicycle was much more in demand by younger unmarried women of the late 1880s, who chose it less as a means of transporation than as a declaration of independence, since it permitted them to move about without a chaperone and at small expense. (Although the initial purchase of a good new bicycle was quite high at £30, second-hand vehicles could be purchased for much less.)[17] Our middle-class married woman, however, being in her late thirties or early forties and no longer young by Victorian standards, probably felt too old and insecure for such strenuous and conspicuous activity.

One popular activity among middle-aged ladies for an afternoon was playing cards, at first on an occasional basis, then regularly. Many of them joined card clubs where, under the pretext of playing bridge, they could get together for gossip, congeniality, and refreshments. By the later decades, card playing in the afternoon was more attuned to her lifestyle than making morning social calls or conducting "At Homes," already falling out of fashion.

It is doubtful that our middle-class matron became much involved in sports, which were being stressed as a means of self-improvement for younger women in the 1890s. The middle-class matron and her husband may have joined a suburban tennis club or gone to a subscription-requiring skating rink, but in those cases the vigorous aspects of such sports were, for the most part, subordinate to the social contact involved.[18] Archery, croquet, and golf, although frequently associated with high society, were also middle-class indulgences.[19]

Meeting friends in London to attend cultural events was surely attempted. Popular concerts of classical music were held in St. James's Hall every Monday evening at eight o'clock and every Saturday afternoon at 3 P.M. during the season,[20] and concerts were also held at the Royal Albert Hall and the Crystal Palace in Sydenham at irregular intervals.[21] Afternoons could be spent vising the Horticultural Society's gardens, or Kew Gardens, or the Zoological Gardens,[22] or going to the National Gallery or the National Portrait Gallery.[23] Just strolling in the park had its pleasant attractions.

However, visiting London for pleasure was not easy to do in the 1880s, since London was just beginning to accommodate itself to seeing respectable women in public without male escorts. The 1880s and early 1890s were periods of adjustment and experimentation, with occasional embarrassment for the women, particularly middle-class matrons who were not accustomed to unpleasant confrontation, and resentment by men at the female effrontery of invading heretofore male precincts.

Until the Aereated Bread Company (A.B.C.) tea shops opened in London in 1880, there were no places to which a middle-class woman could go for a meal, either by herself or with women friends.[24] A popular guide book, *Dickens's Dictionary of London* (1880), stated that ladies without male escorts would have no difficulty in having luncheon in the public room of any large restaurant (provided they avoided passing through the drinking bar to get there),[25] but this probably pertained only to the more expensive restaurants. Large hotels, opening their restaurants to nonresidents, were beginning to encourage female patronage by the 1880s,[26] although, again, their prices may have been prohibitively high as well.

The alternative of meeting friends for lunch or tea closer to home where costs were lower presented the same problem, that of finding a place to eat and chat. While there may have been some public eating places for women in the suburbs, they probably were few and difficult to find.

Another problem that women encountered when coming to the West End from the suburbs was the matter of the availability (or nonavailability) of "comfort stations." In 1884, The Ladies Lavatory Company opened up on Oxford Street, built to correct the situation, but the venture was not particularly successful because, although it filled a need, women found it too embarrassing to use.[27]

By 1880, travel to London for unescorted women was relatively uncomplicated on public surface transportation, as trains, trams, and omnibuses were open to their patronage. They could also travel by underground during the day (if they wanted to risk the soot and the noise of the underground steam engines, which were not replaced by electric ones until 1890); but only a brave woman would have risked being so conspicuous as to take the underground during the hours when men were going to or coming from work. Under stress, the respectable woman could always take a hansom cab, even hailing it from the street if she wished (although ten years earlier it would have been deemed unladylike to do so). But taking a cab was relatively expensive and its use was a measure of last resort.

No matter how many options the older middle-class married woman had for spending her free time, at no time was paid employment one of them. By the late 1880s, younger women were beginning to find employment as retail sales clerks, type-writers in offices, clerks in the civil service, or telephone operators.[28] The middle-class matron might have viewed these all as possible employment opportunities for her daughters, should they want to work before they got married.[29] For herself it was out of the question.

In fact, the activity she enjoyed most was satisfying in all ways. It had a serious purpose, yet was almost indulgent; it wasn't too strenuous yet it kept her active. Restful and pleasant, she engaged in it with lady friends in quiet and elegant surroundings that offered many amenities, under the watchful attention of people who took it as their devoted duty to be as accommodating to her needs as they were alert to her preferences.

What did she do? She went shopping.

NOTES

1. Beeton, *Book of Household Management*, 1–2.
2. This is only a presumption. Nowhere in the literature have I found an explanation of the absense of close sibling, paternal, or maternal ties for a middle-class girl coming from a large urban family. It appears taken as a given that her family was a nuclear unit: herself, her husband, and the children, with no reliance on (or, for that matter, contact with) parents, sisters, or brothers. Branca does state (in *Silent Sisterhood*, 146) that middle-class women, unlike women of the working class, did not have a supportive family or neighborhood structure; but while she attributes the lack of community roots to the family having moved about to so many different residences, she gives no explanation as to why the women lacked family roots—a Victorian anomaly that bears further investigation.
3. White, *Women's Magazines*, 75.
4. Ibid.
5. Ibid., 89–90.
6. Mitchell, *Victorian Britain*, 515–56.
7. Burnett, *Cost of Living*, 244.
8. *Dickens's Dictionary of London*, 160.
9. Burnett, *Cost of Living*, 245.
10. Cruse, *The Victorians and Their Reading* (Boston: Houghton Mifflin, 1962), 333.
11. *Dickens's Dictionary of London*, 158.
12. Amy Cruse, *After the Victorians* (1938; reprint, London: Allen & Unwin, 1971), 14. The description given here, however, is of a reading society in a village.
13. Mitchell, *Daily Life*, 223.
14. Hawks, *Romance of Transport*, 213.
15. Gloag, *Victorian Comfort*, 182.
16. Hawks, *Romance of Transport*, 213.
17. David Rubinstein, "Cycling in the 1890s," in *Victorian Studies* 21 (Autumn 1997): 57.

18. Thompson, *Respectable Society*, 256.
19. Ibid.
20. Karl Baedeker (Firm), *London and Its Environs: Handbook for Travellers* (Leipsic: Karl Baedeker, 1892), 40.
21. Ibid., 40–41.
22. Ibid., 76–77.
23. Ibid.
24. Adburgham, *Shops and Shopping*, 231.
25. *Dickens's Dictionary of London*, 149.
26. Ibid.
27. Weightman and Humphries, *Making of Modern London*, 57.
28. Gloag, *Victorian Comfort*, 190.
29. Gorham, *The Feminine Ideal*, 30.

CHAPTER 15

The Middle-Class Housewife as Shopper: The Emergence of Late-Nineteenth-Century "Consumerism"

After the pressing duties of the house were done, our middle-class married woman boarded a train for London, where she met her friends to spend the afternoon shopping.

Possibly they went to Whiteley's Department Store, in Westbourne Grove, which had opened a refreshment room for the ladies in 1872.[1] Whiteley's had been a drapery establishment in 1863 but began expanding its line of goods soon after that—going from ladies' clothing to gentlemen's outfitting (1869), to tailoring and carrying boots and hats (1872), to stationery (1873), to furniture, china, and glass (1875)—and opening a food department that same year. It also provided dry cleaning services for its customers in 1874, opened a banking department (1875), and even provided a theatre ticket agency in 1879.[2] An anonymous guidebook in 1887 somewhat extravagantly described Whiteley's, the "Universal Provider," as follows:

Whiteley's is an immense symposium of the arts and industries of the nation and of the world; a grand review of everything that goes to make life worth living passing in seemingly endless array before critical but bewildered humanity; an international exhibit of the resources and products of earth and air, flood and field, established as one of the greatest "lions" of the metropolis.[3]

Shopping at a place like this in the late 1880s and 1890s was like nothing the middle-class matron had known in her childhood or early adulthood.

Before she married, when as a young lady she shopped with her mother in the late 1860s and early '70s, retailers selling to the public operated out of small shops. If they were milliners, bootmakers, or tailors, they produced the goods they sold to their customers. If they were haberdashers, grocers, or general dealers, they sold goods purchased earlier from wholesalers or producers.[4] In either case, no shopkeeper bothered to use the shop window to display the goods they carried inside, relying instead on their name and reputation as reputable merchants to attract and retain customers. In fact, the proprietors looked at any evidence of advertisement, or what they termed "puffery," as being in bad taste, something not done by respectable, established tradesmen.[5]

No display of goods appeared inside the store either. The customer came in, took a seat at the counter, and told the shopkeeper what she wanted; he then fetched whatever she asked for, if he had it in stock.[6] If he didn't happen to have what she wanted, that was unfortunate but couldn't be helped.

Because prices were not marked on the goods, the customer always had to ask how much each item cost. Often, after asking to see a number of things, she ended up purchasing the article even if the price was more than she wanted to spend, being too embarrassed to leave without buying.[7]

In general, the attitude of the fixed-shop retailer was not particularly consumer-friendly. While the proprietor was deferential to the wealthy (as was customary everywhere), he did not bother to show the same interest in customers of lesser status. He sold what he carried and implicitly let it be known that the long-time existence of his emporium was proof of his superior knowledge and judgment in stock procurement. Those who protested about his often shoddy goods, high prices, limited stock or indifferent attitude[8] were encouraged to take their custom elsewhere. Under such conditions shopping for clothing or household goods was a necessary but not very pleasant chore.

These conditions still prevailed when the young lady married in the late 1870s. Her opportunities to shop in the more fashionable areas of London before she married (when such shopping might have been exciting) had been comparatively few, considering the chaperonage restrictions and limited finances of her parents. Although she probably was aware of changes taking place in the shopping world by noticing that bigger stores were starting up in many places—both in London and on her own suburban High Street—she had not yet time to explore them. By and large, she continued to shop in the '70s and early '80s as her mother and her grandmother had shopped before her.

But (unknown to her, of course) impersonal market forces operating throughout the century were already producing changes in the distributive trades. By the middle of the century, Britain's manufacturing and large-scale industrial production techniques had spread to many areas, producing a delayed industrial revolution in the manufacture of consumer goods.[9] The boot and shoe industry, men's clothing, and the food industries all had moved on from earlier near-handicraft, small-scale operations to widespread factory mass production.[10] Industries began manufacturing items that carried traditional names but were virtually new products. For the first time previously unknown consumer goods such as factory-made footwear and clothing, patent medicines, margarine, eating chocolate, and cigarettes appeared on the market.[11] The huge upsurge in demand for consumer products rose to such an extent that, for the first time, goods were being produced in anticipation of demand rather than in response to orders.[12]

At the same time, with the decline of British agriculture, a flood of inexpensive, standardized foodstuffs poured into the country from abroad of such magnitude that the traditional sales methods and food trade outlets simply could not handle the volume.[13] A huge unsatisfied demand led to an atmosphere of experimentation and expansion.[14] During this transition period, a handful of innovative proprietors, men with a highly developed business sense and unfettered imaginations, began to develop new ways of attracting consumers, not just accommodating them. Tentatively but inexorably, new techniques of selling, new policies regarding prices and cash flow, and new arrangements of retail stores began to emerge, at first alongside the older established and traditional ones, then in place of them.[15] The department store was coming into its own.

Actually the first British department stores began in the northern cities early in the century. In 1831, two stores in particular, Kendal, Milne & Faulkner ("the Bazaar") of Manchester and Bainbridge in Newcastle, initiated many of the practices later incorporated in the Bon Marché of Paris (which has often been incorrectly cited as the "first" department store).[16] Kendal Milne, for example, was the first store to institute the rule that prices would be marked on all goods so that customers could walk around and look at the items on the counter before committing themselves to buy.[17] This establishment also initiated the periodic sale, at which goods were offered at reduced prices.[18] Eye-catching window displays, with recessed doorways for the maximum showing of products, was another of the Bazaar's innovations.[19]

Bainbridge was the first to expand into a store with a variety of departments under the same roof. In 1845 it was already featuring dress and furnishing fabrics, fashion accessories, furs, family mourning clothes, and "sewed muslin dresses" (an early form of ready-to-wear clothing) and, soon after, a full ready-made clothing department and a men's fabrics department were installed.[20] The gathering of many different lines of goods in one building, each containing a huge variety of sizes, colors, and styles, became the most striking characteristic of the department store.

These large British retail marts evolved, for the most part, from older, already established drapery and clothing shops, although two of them, Harrods and Fortnum & Mason, began as grocery stores. All proliferated in the second half of the century.[21] In London, Thomas Wallis in Holborn, Nicholson's and George Hitchcock in St. Paul's Churchyard, Shoolbred's in Tottenham Court Road, Peter Robinson in Oxford Street, Dickins & Jones in Regent Street, and Swan & Edgar at Piccadilly Circus, to name only some, were all in operation before 1875.[22]

The advent of consumer-oriented retail outlets offering a multiplicity of goods and ranges of selection never seen in the traditional stores was, for shoppers, a wonderful and welcome change.[23] Finding different lines of goods under one roof enabled the consumer for the first time to do her shopping in one place at one time, instead of having to go from one specialized outlet to another.

For the housewife who was particularly price conscious, the department stores offered attractively competitive prices. Their prices were not only below those charged by the traditional stores that aimed to serve a middle-class clientele,[24] but compared favorably to those offered by the two other new retailing centers, Co-operative Societies stores and the Army and Navy Stores, whose principal aim was to attract working-class customers through an emphasis on low prices alone.[25]

For a long while, the department stores' low prices were sufficient to induce the middle-class housewife to shop there even though it often involved a journey out of her home neighborhood. But she continued to shop there even when they stopped pushing a low-price policy (although often they continued to be less expensive than local outlets).[26] In the later decades, the department stores, in shifting their attention to the needs of the middle classes, instituted policies that eventually became more important to these customers than low prices.

The open display of goods in the stores and marking of prices on the goods, allowing the shopper to make on-the-spot price comparisons and judgments, were two innovations that were extremely attractive to the middle-class housewife.[27] Quick delivery guaranteed for all goods purchased was another she appreciated.[28] Some stores in fact adopted the practice (started in the 1840s by Benjamin Hyam & Co. of Liverpool) of allowing their customers to return goods if they were not completely satisfied, assuring them that "any garment bought or taken away, if not satisfactory, will be exchanged, if not worn or injured,"[29] something the more traditional stores never instituted.

One of the most startling departures from traditional selling practices was the department stores' cash-on-purchase policy, in contrast to the almost universal policy followed by big providers of goods to sell on credit.[30] (One notable exception was Harrods, which in 1885 had already modified its predominantly cash-on-purchase policy to permit credit buying for approved customers.)[31]

Although the procedure presumably was established by the retailer in order to avoiding bad-credit losses,[32] the middle-class housewife welcomed the cash-on-purchase idea for her own reasons. The "for cash" policy gave the housewife control, for the first time, over expenditures which she needed to make but, until then, did not have enough money on hand to buy. Having hard cash in her pocketbook to spend as she saw fit, she now was able to exercise personal judgment in the matter of spending rather than having her purchases under the constant overview of her husband, the controller of the checkbook.

But the most compelling feature of the new department

stores, the overwhelming attraction that brought the middle-class married woman returning to them over and over again, was their new and refreshing consumer-friendly attitude. The stores' persistent affirmation of the concept that "the customer is always right" encouraged these Victorian matrons to browse often and spend freely, knowing that, if they were not totally pleased with their purchases, satisfactory accommodation would always be made.

Departing from established retailing practices, these store proprietors now openly solicited a customer's total patronage, anxious that she should not only purchase clothing and foodstuffs from them but also large items such as household appliances and other devices and services.[33] To this end, they deferred to her wishes, listened to what she said she wanted, ordered goods she asked for if the items were not in stock, and informed her promptly when the goods were available.[34]

While catering to the housewife's shopping wishes, the stores also introduced features that made shopping itself a pleasurable experience. They set up conveniences as tea shops, lunch rooms, lounges, writing rooms and "retiring rooms" (lavatories), all to allow the woman to rest and chat with her friends and, later, perhaps do more shopping.[35] In fact, by offering women amenities they could find nowhere else, these stores provided them with an experience, amid elegant ambience, similar to that which clubs provided for men.

The array of goods on attractive display, offered in overwhelming variety, was extremely alluring, making the shopping experience a heady one. In the words of one observer, the London department store turned out to be more than just a collection of things to buy:

[It became] a total alternative environment, a vision of abundance, a succession of surprises, a place to go to be cosseted, flattered, and amused. . . . A meeting place and promenade, a home away from home . . . [yet] it served less to rival the home than to complement it, providing ideas and opportunities for domestic embellishments.[36]

Our middle-class matron, though flattered by all this luxury and temptation, was not overwhelmed by it. She was still governed, to the core, by her middle-class sense of thrift and proportion.

Of all the appealing aspects of the department store, the one of greatest attraction to the middle-class housewife was her sense that, for the first time, men in charge were seriously listening to her opinions. In these places she could speak directly to a floor walker or store manager, suggesting (though in muted tones) various improvements she felt were needed—with the expectation that they would be seriously considered. It was extremely gratifying to her to find that important business people were willing to take her ideas seriously—and when they did, she reciprocated with her patronage, making the department store her retail outlet of choice.

By the last quarter of the century, it was evident that the middle-class housewife wanted much more than just *things* to improve the quality of life for herself and her family, although aids to make household chores easier were high on her list. (As a result, while many of the large appliances she wanted were not yet on the market, stores began to stock a huge array of new kitchen gadgets and tools, such as apple corers, potato parers, egg beaters, flour sifters and standardized measuring cups and spoons, to make work in the kitchen less tedious.)[37] But she wanted more.

She wanted relief from sewing and kitchen work—and department stores responded with lines of ready-made clothing so she wouldn't have to do so much sewing, and prepackaged, brand-name goods to free her from having to make things "from scratch." (In fact, it was the eye-catching advertising layouts in the women's magazines that made her conscious of specific brands of goods available in the stores, inducing her to come into the shops to ask for the advertised products.)[38]

When she articulated a wish for more recreational goods and services for herself and her family and for indulgences of various kinds, the stores provided these as well. In a department store, for example, could be found elaborate and exotic food departments, a travel booking agency, a banking department, a theatre ticket agency, a catering service (known in Whiteley's as their "hire and exhibitions" department), a railway ticket agency, and even a laundry,[39] all in one building, with satisfaction (and delivery) guaranteed.

Our housewife spent a great deal of time shopping. Without realizing it, shopping connoted more to her than just buying things. Between the middle-class married woman and the department store there developed an unspoken but deep symbiotic relationship, all the more binding because neither the customer nor the provider had the slightest idea that so subjective a relationship even existed.

NOTES

1. Olsen, *Growth of Victorian London*, 124.
2. Ibid., 122, 124.
3. Ibid., 122, quoting from the guidebook.
4. Jefferys, *Retail Trading*, 2.
5. Ibid., 4.
6. Mitchell, *Daily Life*, 132.
7. Ibid.
8. Jefferys, *Retail Trading*, 4–5.
9. Ibid., 8.
10. Ibid.
11. Ibid., 35.
12. Ibid., 8.
13. Ibid., 8.
14. Ibid., 9.
15. Ibid., 6.
16. Adburgham, *Shops and Shopping*, 137.
17. Ibid., 138.
18. Ibid.
19. Ibid.
20. Ibid., 139–40.

21. Ibid., 171.
22. Ibid., 142–43.
23. Jefferys, *Retail Trading*, 20.
24. Ibid.
25. Ibid., 18.
26. Ibid., 20.
27. Ibid., 37.
28. Ibid., 20; also Mitchell, *Daily Life*, 132.
29. Adburgham, *Shops and Shopping*, 140–41.
30. Mitchell, *Victorian Britain*, 720.
31. Adburgham, *Shops and Shopping*, 234.
32. Mitchell, *Daily Life*, 132.
33. Olsen, *Growth of Victorian London*, 124.
34. Ibid.
35. Mitchell, *Daily Life*, 132–33.
36. Olsen, *Growth of Victorian London*, 124.
37. DuVall, *Domestic Technology*, 126.
38. White, *Women's Magazines*, 65–68.
39. Olsen, *Growth of Victorian London*, 124.

PART III

THE END OF THE CENTURY: CONCLUSION

CHAPTER 16

London in 1900: A World City Reluctant to Change

The nineteenth century slipped imperceptibly into the twentieth. On January 1, 1900, in the classified ads of the London *Times* (printed traditionally on the first page of the paper), a small ad indicated that a story written by a Mr. H. G. Wells, *Love and Mr. Lewisham*, would be found in the *Times* weekly edition. A large display ad on the same page announced that the Grand Christmas Show, starring the Greatest Circus Artists and Novelties in Europe, was still showing at the Crystal Palace.[1]

Page three printed summaries of some of the year's economic news: a review on agriculture for the past year, an estimate of land and property sales for 1899 ("the tone of the real estate market of the year just closing has been altogether very satisfactory"), and an accounting of the revenue of the United Kingdom for various periods as compared to the same periods in the previous year.

The ongoing Boer War in South Africa dominated the foreign news, starting on page five, featuring the latest intelligence reports from the war front. Judging from the messages about the siege of Ladysmith in Natal (which would continue for two more months until lifted at the end of February) and from the Cape Colony, the southern frontier, the western frontier, Delagoa Bay, and the Colonial contingents (Canadian and Indian)—the army's situation was not good.

Other foreign news included articles on German-English relations, on France, Austro-Hungary, the Papal Nuncio, India, and the United States ("prosperity, stock values not affected")—but, except for a suggestion of trouble in the article on Germany, nothing in current events hinted at the catastrophe that would overwhelm the nation in another fifteen years. The old Queen, who had celebrated her Diamond Jubilee three years before at the age of seventy-eight, was still on the throne; not until 1901 did the Victorian Age officially conclude with her death on January 22 of that year.

On January 1, 1900, England was the same as it was the day before, with little perceptible change anywhere, least of all in London.

By the turn of the century, Greater London's population was enormous: four and a half million in the administrative counties, over two million more in the "outer ring," and still more people in the contiguous urban areas, running deep into Kent and Surrey, almost to the boundaries of Middlesex.[2] In the previous thirty years, it had grown faster than any of the largest provincial urban areas and far faster than the national population as a whole.[3] By 1900, London contained one-fifth of the entire population of England and Wales.[4] It was by then the largest most populous city in the entire world.

But the story of London as a world-city (both as a soaring imaginative construct as well as in actual accomplishments) must be told elsewhere. Here we look at it more prosaically, if somewhat superficially, paying attention to its physical and technological features as perhaps a tourist might—or as a middle-class matron well into middle-age might see the city she had known all her life.

From all outward appearances, the London of tourist attractions, galleries, architectural residences and palaces, shops and arcades, parks and squares remained as before. Even its principal thoroughfares in the business and commercial heart of the city appeared visually the same. While the widening of some streets had taken place in the last half of the nineteenth century,[5] and the roads appeared somewhat cleaner and more orderly due to the efforts of a multiplicity of local and county authorities concerned with municipal housekeeping,[6] two retrogressive features (in contrast to large cities elsewhere) were obvious: the streets were still lighted by gas (no electric street lamps) and vehicular traffic, as congested as ever, was still horse-drawn with hardly a motor car are in sight.

The lack of electric lighting on the streets was truly an anomaly. Electric lighting in private industry, businesses, and commercial establishments became a part of British modern life almost as soon as the incandescent electric lamp was invented (almost simultaneously, but independently, in 1878 and 1879, by Joseph Wilson Swan in England and Thomas Alva Edison in America). By 1880 electric lights were installed in the machine rooms of the London *Times* and in Albert Hall, the British Museum, and Victoria Station.[7] The streets of other English cities such as Liverpool, Bristol, and Brighton were all lit by electricity by the 1880s.[8] But the movement to install electric lamps in the streets of London proceeded very slowly, with only 200 of the 2,000 miles of London streets and roads having them by 1900.[9] Not until the eve of the Great War were the city streets fully electrified.

Horse-drawn vehicles continued to be ubiquitous. Although cable-hauled trams had come to Great Britain from America in 1884 as a way to get the horses off the street, the principal cities to adopt that form of transportation were Birmingham and Edinburgh,[10] not London. By the early 1890s, the electric trolley was in wide use in Germany, the Low Countries, and the United States,[11] with fast, efficient electric trams running on the streets of Brussels, Frankfurt, Cologne, and Berlin by 1897.[12] London continued to have horse-drawn council trams north of the Thames until 1905.[13]

There were still almost no internal combustion engine automobiles to be seen, even though Gottfried Daimler had patented a high-speed internal combustion engine in 1885 and 1886,[14] and Rudolph Diesel had taken out a British patent in 1892.[15] One reason was that, in 1865, fearing the dangers of steam-powered vehicles racing down the roads, Parliament passed the Red Flag Act, requiring that all power-driven vehicles travelling on public highways be preceded by a man in front waving a red flag, thus effectively limiting a vehicle's maximum speed to that of the walking man, four miles per hour.[16] This law was not repealed until 1896.

Finally, in 1895, in anticipation of the repeal of this law, a steam-driven phaeton and a four-wheeled petroleum-propelled carriage appeared on the streets of London,[17] the latter capable of travelling, it was said, at the amazing speed of "fifteen miles an hour on the flat and as much as four miles an hour uphill."[18] Although the Prince of Wales took a ride in a motor car in 1896 after the Red Flag Act was repealed to give the seal of royal approval to the gasoline-driven vehicle,[19] acceptance of the motor car was slow, with widespread protests throughout the country (possibly not spontaneous) against the dust the machine raised, the horses it frightened, and the dangers of its high speed.[20] Not until the first decade of the twentieth century were private automobiles to be seen in any appreciable numbers in Great Britain. It was not until 1905 that internal-combustion motor omnibuses begin to supplant horse traction on London streets,[21] with motor cabs coming into service in 1907.

In 1898 and 1899 private electrically driven carriages had begun to appear.[22] But few steam-powered cars or electric 'buses were to be found on the London streets until 1897, when a few electric-powered 'buses made their appearance (in contrast to the use of electric 'buses in the provinces and Scotland since 1877).[23]

By 1895, however, a human-powered vehicle was seen everywhere, although more in the city parks and suburban lanes than on the city streets: the safety bicycle. Although technically invented some twenty years earlier (in a different form), the bicycle did not gain great popularity until the last decade of the century.[24]

Although the bicycle initially was used in London by small tradesmen as a delivery vehicle,[25] its major impact on urban and suburban living was related to the consumer market. The vehicle gave individuals mobility they had not experienced before, since it was both individually controlled and relatively inexpensive. It was particularly welcomed by young adults as a means of making social interaction between the sexes easier; and by 1900, it had become a common means of transport for men and women alike.[26]

In communications, however, London showed a zest for technological modernization, with the rapid spread of innovations in the last quarter of the century. In commerce and government, the telegraph was now being supplemented (and in some cases supplanted) by the new voice-transmitting device, the telephone, invented in 1876 and found in business establishments throughout the city by 1881,[27] although long-distance lines linking London to Manchester, Liverpool, and Birmingham were not put into place until 1890.[28] However, the telephone's use in private homes was, by the end of the century, still only for the wealthy. New consumer-directed electrical machines for entertainment also appeared on the market: the phonograph and gramophone "talking machines" for the home,[29] and electrically run visual devices for public use before audiences. One such machine, as mentioned before, was in operation at the Empire theatre in March of 1895, and another at the same time at the Alhambra theatre. Both projected a series of images on a screen that seemed to move—the first motion pictures.[30]

Another revolutionary instrument, although manually operated, made its appearance in private and government offices throughout the city: the typewriter. Invented by Christopher Sholes and manufactured and distributed in Britain by E.

Remington (the firearms manufacturer) when the Remington Typewriter Company opened the first British dealership in 1886, the machine became commonplace and often essential to every office except the very smallest by 1900.[31]

The typewriter's introduction, it might be noted, had ramifications far beyond its utility as a business tool. Because it was operated primarily by women from the very beginning,[32] its rapid and widespread adoption in business, government, and commerce revolutionized the character of employment in the city. Once the civil service and businesses began hiring women as "type-writers" (i.e., persons who wrote by machine rather than by hand) in the 1880s, women flocked to enter the employment marketplace, eager to avail themselves of respectable white-collar work.[33] An unintentional but concomitant result of the influx of women into the job market as type-writers, shop assistants, and clerks was a noticeable reduction in the pool of women the wealthier middle-class and upper-class matrons had always relied upon to furnish them domestic servants.[34] As a result, perhaps, mechanical domestic labor-savings devices suddenly became very popular with upper-class matrons who found themselves increasingly deprived of human labor-saving devices: servants.

By the last decade of the century, also, London had finally altered its structure of government to provide for better representation. According to one historian, the "substitution of elected county councils for the ancient administration of counties by the justices of the peace at quarter sessions was a substitution of the democratic for the aristocratic principle."[35] But to say this was not to concede much. The city, even under broader democratic control, was not able to bring about the important local reforms that so many other British cities managed to do.[36] None of its administrative government agencies seemed able to systematically deal with the city's many problems, and any private attempts at reform "always broken down in the face of the stubborn resistance of vested interests."[37] In 1900, for example, water distribution in the municipality still remained in the hands of eight or nine private monopolies, gas supplies were controlled by three noncompeting companies, and little positive action was taken to develop new services, such as public libraries, for the residents.[38]

The new century lay ahead, but for the moment there was no sense of urgency to modernize. There was plenty of time in the coming years to make whatever changes were necessary, both in the private realm and in public actions, to add to what had already been accomplished—or so it seemed on January 1, 1900.

NOTES

1. London *Times*, January 1, 1900, 1. The same source was used for the information in the following three paragraphs, on the various pages named in the text.
2. Briggs, *Victorian Cities*, 312.
3. Ibid.
4. Dyos and Reeder, "Slums and Suburbs," 362.
5. *Encyclopedia Britannica*, 11th ed., vol. 16, 944.
6. Besant, *London in the Nineteenth Century*, 346.
7. Mitchell, *Daily Life*, 81.
8. Alan Bott, *Our Fathers, 1870–1900: Manners and Customs of the Ancient Victorians* (London: Heinemann, 1931), 207 (published in America as *This Was England* [Garden City, N.Y.: Doubleday, 1932]).
9. Besant, *London in the Nineteenth Century*, 325, 346.
10. Ensor, *England, 1870–1914*, 280.
11. Ibid., 280–81.
12. Ibid., 281.
13. Ibid.
14. Ibid.
15. Mitchell, *Victorian Britain*, 786.
16. Allen, *Victorian England, 1850–1900*, 191.
17. Bott, *Our Fathers*, 220.
18. Ibid., 221.
19. Bott and Clephane, *Our Mothers*, 17.
20. Bott, *Our Fathers*, 109.

21. *Encyclopedia Britannica*, 11th ed., vol. 16, 944.
22. Allen, *Victorian England, 1850–1900*, 192.
23. Hart, *English Life in the Nineteenth Century*, ch. 2; also Mitchell, *Victorian Britain*, 813.
24. Rubinstein, "Cycling in the 1890s," 47.
25. Ibid., 51.
26. Ibid., 55.
27. Gloag, *Victorian Comfort*, 194.
28. Bott, *Our Fathers*, 209.
29. Ibid., 205.
30. Metcalf, *Victorian London*, 169.
31. Mitchell, *Victorian Britain*, 826.
32. Ibid.
33. McBride, *Domestic Revolution*, 115, 116.
34. Ibid., 116.
35. Ensor, *England, 1870–1914*, 294–95.
36. Briggs, *Victorian Cities*, 320.
37. Ibid., 320.
38. Ibid., 322–24.

CHAPTER 17

The Middle-Class Housewife in 1900: Inadvertent Agent for Change

For the middle-class matron, the slip from the nineteenth into the twentieth century was also imperceptible (not counting any celebration she and her husband may have enjoyed to mark the new millennium). If she had seen the *Times* on January 1, she may have thought fleetingly about Mr. Wells only if his name had been mentioned among her book-club lady friends as an author of note. The advertisement about the Grand Christmas Show may have revived a brief recollection of visits to the circus with the children in the past, nothing more.

Her feelings about the Boer War would have been acute only if she had a son in the army (one born in the late 1870s); for while military service was never a middle-class occupation, this war for the first time saw many middle-class young men volunteering to serve their country.[1] Otherwise, in reading the news, she only felt the same unease and concern of everyone in the nation, including the old Queen (who was still on the throne and would remain there for another year), on how poorly the brave English troops were faring.

On the eve of the twentieth century, if she saw her London

with the eyes of a tourist, she would also have been unhappy with the uneven state of municipal progress, primarily for reasons of national pride. By then she would have taken a Thomas Cook tour to Europe and seen the efficient trams on the streets of Berlin[2] (which London still did not have) and the amazing horseless carriages on the roads of Paris[3] (still rare to nonexistent in London).

Governmental reluctance to modernize may have made her uncomfortable for another reason: it seemed too similar to what she had been witnessing on the domestic scene for years. Knowing how long it was taking technology to address domestic needs, the middle-class matron could easily have found herself strongly, if silently, on the side of progress on the municipal front as well.

We now take a final look at our lovely MCMW living in London and married for some twenty-five years. She was now about fifty years old, an "old" woman, according to the demographics. How did she occupy her daily hours in 1900?

We can draw a word picture of her as a "representative" middle-class married woman only if we presume that certain changes had *not* taken place; had any of these occurred, her pattern of life would have been greatly distorted, forcing major alterations in her lifestyle. A death in the family, for example, depriving her of an adequante income, would have been one such disasterous occurence. Similarly the death or removal of any of her children upon whom she and her husband depended for financial support or for physical care would have been another. Unexpected economic reverses for the family would have been still another, causing a sharp loss in income or status level: a calamitous event. The onset of grave physical or mental disease or disability striking either her husband or herself (or, for that matter, one of the children under her care) would have caused a major dislocation, necessitating adjustments in living that constituted a difference in kind, not just degree.

Barring these possibilities, presuming that all outward circumstances continued to be favorable (or at least not drastically altered), the matron's environment and activities at century's end can be projected with some degree of certainty.

The family was still in slightly straited circumstances. Although her husband's income may have risen (although routine incremental increases of salary based on longevity were not the norm), so had their expenses gone up, absorbing surplus income.

More expensive housing was certainly one such increased expense. The house in which they now lived was not the one they rented in 1875. By 1900, they had "removed" a number of times, each time advancing to better (and more expensive) quarters in improved surroundings and a more prestigious location, in keeping with the family's rise in income and status.[4]

If the house they now occupied was of the type that architects had begun building in the nineties, its most obvious improvement was a kitchen that had been raised from the basement to the ground floor, closer to the dining room.[5] If not, the house had undergone renovation including the introduction of a commodity lift (if only a cumbersome hand-operated device), connecting the basement to the upper floors, allowing servants to bring food and fuel to the higher floors without stair-climbing.[6]

Architects and builders were also experimenting with various schemes for including more baths into middle-class homes, although one innovation of putting them in dressing rooms where clothes were hung eventually had to be abandoned because of the excessive dampness.[7] But baths were now found in separate rooms. Also, gas outlets for lighting and appliances were in most rooms of the house.

Furnishings had gradually changed over the years. The ponderous furniture so appropriate from 1875 to 1880 had been replaced with pieces of lighter design,[8] and the heavy crimson drapery and dark wallpaper replaced by lighter colors. (However, this matron probably was not enthusiastic about a decorating trend fashionable in the late 1890s that applied vivid colors—such as peacock greens and blues, magentas, violets, and pinks—everywhere, according to one home furnishing critic, "with more enthusiasm than discrimination.")[9]

But sitting and living room furniture was still chosen for lounging rather than grace of design.[10] The popular easy chair with a high back and side shoulders (the so-called "grandfather" chair)[11] continued to appeal, as did upholstery of slightly explosive plumpness, looking, as the same critic observed, "like the paunch of a stout man protesting against the restraint of a waistcoat."[12] Over the years, furniture fashions came and went, some more radical than others, some in better taste than others; judging from their past behavior, the now-elderly couple tended to favor the familiar rather than the innovative in home furnishings.

Of all the rooms, the kitchen had changed the most; it was there that advances in domestic technology were most evident. The coal range had given way to a gas appliance. The Gas, Light & Coke Company (the largest of the three gas companies in London) effectively introduced gas appliances into the middle-class kitchen through the medium of advertising, stressing the comfort advantage, particularly in summer, of using a gas stove instead of a heat-producing coal range.[13] The company also used innovative promotions such as renting out the commercial gas stoves to customers instead of insisting they buy them and introducing the coin-in-the-slot gas meter for householders with budgetary concerns.[14] The gas companies held exhibitions and cookery lectures for housewives, maintained well-stocked showrooms, and personally canvassed potential customers, concentrating specifically on the middle class.[15] So successful were they in selling their stoves that, in 1898, one out of every four households supplied with gas had a gas cooker,[16] with one particular model, the "Charing Cross Kitchener," remaining popular well into the twentieth century.[17]

Electric power companies were not able to compete with gas companies for middle-class custom. Electricity remained so much more expensive than gas that its use was far more common among the wealthy than in moderate-income households.[18] Moreover electrical appliances remained of questionable quality. Although in 1890 the General Electric Company heavily promoted an "electric rapid cooking apparatus that boiled a pint of water in 12 minutes," the early stoves used a great deal of current with heating elements that burned out quickly. Not until the new century, when nickel-chromium resistance wire appeared, could the heating units be perfected.[19] Similarly in 1882 an electric iron came on the market, but it was very dangerous to use; safe electric irons were not available for another twenty years.[20] Other electric-driven appliances that housewives rely upon today, such as the vacuum cleaner, an easy-to-use clothes-washing machine, and domestic food refrigerators, were not yet on the market.[21]

Although many Londoners still relied upon fireplaces for heating, by century's end rooms were more often heated by some version of the enclosed, coal-fueled Franklin stove (often hidden behind camouflaging façades or tucked away into the fireplace area).[22] But even these were being replaced by gas space heaters. (However, and this is a British peculiarity, central heating was not to be found then in any British home, not even those of the wealthy. Central heating did not find a ready market until some fifty years later, after World War II.)

By the end of the century, flush toilets in separate rooms were at last usual in the middle-class home. The reason the installation of such devices took so long was less a lack of ingenuity than the lack of coordination. Toilets could not be installed until houses were equipped with proper flushing facilities, also drainage pipes that carried off the effluent had to be hooked up to municipal sewage systems. These had to be installed away from the domestic drinking or washing water supply that might be contaminated (which also had to be drawn out of the house into a city water-drainage system). Too often, if the water closet was put in improperly by inexperienced workmen, water overflowed into rainpipes or down dressing-room windows.[23] Even when a new drainage system was installed, the stench of the old cesspool often continued to seep through the house. Sometimes sewers blocked up after rains, exuding offensive odors; in dry weather the odor from the muck was equally bad.[24] To get an odorless and sanitary drainage system into the Victorian home, to get water closets, bathtubs and spigot-fitted sinks all operating properly required many separate elements to be in place at the same time and properly coordinated. Even by 1900, finding such plumbing advances in the middle-class homes of London could not be taken for granted.

By the late 1890s, the MCMW probably no longer did the hard work involved in housework, partly because she now had servants to do it, but also because she may no longer have been physically able. Also, ideas of what caring for the home entailed had changed, with many scrubbing routines being dropped and a "rationalization" of cooking and housework lightening the domestic load considerably.[25]

The housewife had now acquired a second housemaid, although this second full-time servant probably replaced the nursemaid who earlier had taken care of the young children and did housecleaning besides. By then she would also have hired a cook to prepare the meals and do the day-to-day marketing. By 1900 it was easier to hire and keep a cook because kitchens were better designed and the number of courses and the extravagance of the recipes had lessened from earlier years.[26] But the matron continued to do some food and grocery marketing, buying the food at the well-stocked department stores where she regularly shopped.

The housewife continued as clothing manager, but not as seamstress. For a while in the 1880s, handling the family clothing required more rather than less of her time when, as seamstress, she personally sewed much of the family's clothing instead of having others do the work. But by the nineties, ready-to-wear clothing was available in such a great variety of styles, sizes, and prices that she abandoned her sewing role and simply shopped for ready-mades.

The woman's role as employer, although now expanded to cover three live-in servants and whatever temporary help was necessary, probably was less burdensome than earlier both because she had acquired more experience in handling the help without conflict and also because many of the irksome jobs simply had been dropped.[27]

We do not know whether the matron's financial management role had changed in the 1890s. As the husband's income increased, family expenditures also increased, and his own leisure and family recreational interests expanded. It seems likely that the man would have taken over the major money management in the family. However, there appears to have been no research done in this area, and we do not know how financial management was allocated or exercised.

Child-care duties in the family faded with the passing years. The matron stopped having babies and the children graduated from the nursery to the tutelage of outside teachers.

Family health needs continued to occupy the housewife's attention, now revolving about her husband's welfare and her own, as the two passed from middle into old age.[28]

Social duties involving the children now related primarily to enlarging her daughters' matrimonial prospects, although this responsibility was more muted than her mother's had been. Of course the girls were still not yet old enough to make this matter one of real concern—at any rate, the matron's options in channeling her daughters' contacts had become decidedly limited. By century's end, the girls, as teenagers or young adults, were working as shop girls, attending secretarial school or working in an office. Even if they did not work and remained at home, they were making independent contacts through their bicycle or social clubs, close chaperonage being a thing of the past. If the middle-class matron chose to directionalize her daughters' interests, it would have been by making sure the mixed-sex activities sponsored by her church or chapel or by the suburban social group to which she and her husband belonged were so attractive that the daughters would volunatarily turn in that direction.

As home responsibilities waned, the matron spent more time in outside activities. Charitable work continued to be important as it had been for some years; in fact her participation may have increased.[29] She was just as likely to indulge in socializing with women friends, perhaps joining a book club, or playing cards with them, or going to popular cultural activities together.

Shopping continued to be a particularly enjoyable leisure-time activity. Free afternoons were regularly spent with friends browsing through their favorite department stores, looking about, chatting, snacking in the refreshment rooms, possibly buying something, content at the end of the day to return home to her family.

The middle-class married woman's life remained, as from the beginning, centered on family and home. This did not mean that she was unaware of the political or social movements that stirred the country, such as the war in South Africa, the stirrings among the working classes, or even the ideas of the New Women. However, these were subjects for conversation rather than events that involved her directly. Her housewifery interests had a much smaller focus, one that was to her infinitely more important.

Yet, within the parameters of her circumscribed private life, the MCMW showed an irrepressible preference for modernization and a powerful, if unarticulated, reproof of those who refused to change.[30] This leaning appeared to have inadvertently helped the nation alter its attitude towards change and modernization.[31]

The housewife's awareness of the need for change began with her first-hand knowledge of the drudgery of housework, as has been detailed earlier. Although originally conditioned to accept her heavy domestic chores as an obligation of marriage, her early work alongside her servant in cleaning house, doing the laundry, preparing the meals and marketing for food showed her how time-consuming and back-breaking was the work, how inadequate were the tools and facilities available to do it all. Although she had no idea what could be done, she must have felt that there had to be a better way; managing a house was extraordinarily difficult when the house ruled the housewife rather than the other way around.

Her role as an employer reinforced this conviction. Although initially she had little sympathy for the servant's complaints of hard work and inconvenience, she must have recognized through personal experience in doing "servant work" how many of their complaints were justified. For a while she thought that having more money to hire more servants would solve the problem, but hiring more servants, she later discovered, had other drawbacks. Eventually it became clear that the basic difficulty was a poorly planned house, inadequate household aids, and antiquated attitudes. If only the rooms were better arranged, with better light, or fewer stairs, or lighter brooms or mops, or *less work*, the servants would be less cantankerous, more willing to do their jobs, and less likely to leave her employment—making her own job as manager easier.

When amenities eventually appeared that reduced the labor of housework (piped hot water, bright gas-jet lighting in the kitchen and the public rooms, closed stoves for heating that eliminated the mess of open fireplaces, a gas range in the kitchen, flushing water closets, separate rooms for bathtubs with faucets, a kitchen built on the ground floor to be nearer to the dining room, the development of kitchen gadgets to make food preparation easier and quicker), she was delighted and convinced more than ever that technology and change were entirely to her benefit.

How she would have relished reading a book published seventeen years later, in 1917, called *The Labour-Saving*

House! In it the author, Dorothy Peel, put forth her own ideas for making the home friendlier and housekeeping simpler including, among other suggestions, the elimination of coal fires for heating, domestic training courses for servants, simplified meals such as casseroles, linoleum with rubber treads on all the stairs, the use of a suction cleaner and a Bissell carpet sweeper, and glass tops on sideboards and tables to make their cleaning easier.[32]

The advantages of technology were most obvious in the management of the family clothing, as explained in a previous chapter. Others with money to hire capable seamstresses might wax nostalgic about the beauty of hand-made clothing and delicate hand embroidery; but as far as this matron was concerned, the difference in time and cost between making clothing by hand (by herself or outside help) or doing it mechanically was reason enough to unequivocally opt for the sewing machine and, later, to embrace with enthusiasm the advent of ready-made clothes.

The matron was quick to recognize how new inventions had broadened the horizons for the entire family, and particularly for her girls. The safety bicycle now offered more freedom of individual transportation, the telephone and typewriter in the business world were creating respectable jobs that her daughters could hold before settling down into marriage, and (a really heady glimpse into the future) the new horseless carriages actually promised to eliminate the muck and smell that made housekeeping so unpleasant. These new machines also opened up previously unknown vistas that would allow families to travel about more easily, in greater comfort, and at less cost than in horse-drawn conveyances and offering more convenience and less restrictions than train travel.

There were also the darker experiences that reinforced the matron's insistence on change, linked to her own dreadful dealings with the medical profession in the past (as has been detailed earlier). The same fears surfaced as, with advancing age, she found herself again dependent on doctors, seeing that their continued disinclination to embrace new ideas possibly endangered her life and that of her husband.

In all, nothing in the housewife's experience convinced her that there was any advantage in clinging to the old-fashioned ways rather than pushing for change in order to improve life for herself and her family. As far as she was concerned, the modernization process was without question a liberating one.[33]

This attitude was all the more surprising in that it came from a subclass which ordinarily would have supported tradition. Unlike political advocates, social reformers or New Women feminists, the middle-class housewife had no articulated program for change and little inclination to support those who advocated one. Still her inchoate dissatisfaction with the way things were and her conviction that things could be made better was manifest in all her actions. The potency of so inexorable a force cannot be underestimated.

Because of the middle-class woman's positive stance in favor of innovation and change, the process of modernization progressed far more rapidly than it would otherwise have done.[34] In inadvertently becoming an engine for change, she altered the nation's perception of the future and became a significant element in preparing Great Britain for entry into the twentieth century.

NOTES

1. Macqueen-Pope, *Twenty Shillings*, 318.
2. Ensor, *England, 1870–1914*, 280.
3. Ibid.; also Bott, *Our Fathers*, 209.
4. Thompson, *Respectable Society*, 171.
5. Ralph Dutton, *The Victorian Home: Some Aspects of Nineteenth-Century Taste and Manners* (London: B. T. Batsford, 1954), 188.
6. Ibid.
7. Ibid., 189.
8. Gloag, *Victorian Comfort*, 42.
9. Ibid., 48

10. Ibid., 60, 61.
11. Ibid., 66.
12. Ibid., 69–70.
13. See ad in Beeton's *Book of Household Management* (1880 ed.), end of book.
14. Besant, *Life in the Nineteenth Century*, 322; also DuVall, *Domestic Technology*, 115.
15. Davidson, *A Woman's Work*, 67.
16. Ibid.
17. Ibid., 65.
18. Ibid., 68.
19. DuVall, *Domestic Technology*, 116.
20. Wilson, *Life in a Victorian House*, 31.
21. Davidson, *A Woman's Work*, 38.
22. See illustrations in Gloag, *Victorian Comfort*, 111, 112, 115, 117.
23. Wohl, *Endangered Lives*, 1.
24. Ibid.
25. Davidson, *A Woman's Work*, 176.
26. Ibid.
27. Ibid.
28. Wohl, *Endangered Lives*, 328, re. life expectancy.
29. See Lewis, 92–95, *Women in England*, on the MCMW's extended philanthropic role in the late nineteenth century.
30. The thesis developed here, independently arrived at, parallels one put forth by Patricia Branca and Peter N. Stearns in *Modernization of Women in the Nineteenth Century*, The Forum Series (St. Charles, Mo.: Forum Press, 1973), and its later revision, "Middle-class Women and Modernization," chapter 8 in Branca's *Silent Sisterhood*, 144–53.
31. Branca, *Silent Sisterhood*, 150.
32. Mrs. C. S. [Dorothy] Peel, *The Labour-Saving House* (London: John Lane, 1917), 31–32, 49.
33. Branca and Stearns, *Modernization of Women*, 3.
34. Branca, *Silent Sisterhood*, 150.

Appendix: Victorian Money

For the benefit of American readers, the following is a table of late nineteenth-century English currency, replaced in 1971 by a decimal system similar to that used in the United States. The old system was based on the penny, the shilling, and the pound, although there were other coins in circulation, some used throughout the nineteenth and into the twentieth century, others just in the earlier Victorian years.

Name	symbol	equivalency	metal
penny (pl.: pence)	d.		copper [bronze after 1860]
shilling	s.	12 pence	silver
pound (sovereign coin)	£	20 shillings	gold
guinea		£1 1 s.	[not minted after 1813]

Almost all money circulating was in coin, even when transactions involved large sums of money. The smallest paper money issued was the five-pound bank note. Checks were not commonly accepted in ordinary transactions, even in the last quarter of the century.[1]

A pound was literally one pound of gold; it could be weighed on a scale.[2] A Bank of England five-pound bank note was convertible on demand into gold coins.[3]

NOTES

1. Mitchell, *Victorian Britain*, 510.
2. Macqueen-Pope, *Twenty Shillings*, 19.
3. Mitchell, *Victorian Britain*, 510.

Bibliography

CITED REFERENCES

Adburgham, Alison. *Shops and Shopping, 1800–1914: Where and in What Manner the Well-Dressed Englishwoman Bought Her Clothes.* London: Allen & Unwin, 1964.

Allbutt, Henry Arthur. *The Wife's Handbook: How a Woman Should Order Herself During Pregnancy, in the Lying-in Room, and After Delivery, with Hints on the Management of the Baby and Other Matters of Importance Necessary to be Known by Married Women.* 7th ed. London: R. Forder, 1888.

Allen, Arthur Bruce. *Victorian England, 1850–1900: The Complete Background Book.* London: Rockliff, 1956.

Avery, Gillian. *Victorian People in Life and Literature.* New York: Holt, Rinehart & Winston, 1970.

Banks, J. A., and Olive Banks. *Feminism and Family Planning in Victorian England.* Liverpool: Liverpool University Press, 1964.

Beetham, Margaret. *A Magazine of Her Own? Domesticity and Desire in the Woman's Magazine, 1800–1914.* London: Routledge, 1996.

Beeton, Isabella Mary. *Book of Household Management [and] a*

Guide to Cookery in All Branches. London: Ward, Lock & Co., 1861. Also 1880, 1909 eds.
Bentley, Nicholas. *The Victorian Scene: A Picture Book of the Period, 1837–1901.* London: Weidenfeld & Nicolson, 1968.
Besant, Walter. *London in the Nineteenth Century.* 1909. Reprint, New York: Garland, 1985.
Blackwell, Elizabeth. *How to Keep a Household in Health.* London: W. W. Head, 1870.
Blumenfeld, R. D. *R.D.B.'s Diary, 1887–1914.* London: Heinemann, 1930.
Booker, Beryl Lee. *Yesterday's Child, 1890–1909.* London: John Long, 1937.
Booth, Charles, et al. *Life and Labour of the People of London.* 8 vols. London: Macmillan, 1903.
Bott, Alan. *Our Fathers, 1870–1900: Manners and Customs of the Ancient Victorians.* London: Heinemann, 1931. [Published in America as *This Was England.* Garden City, N.Y.: Doubleday, 1932.]
Bott, Alan, and Irene Clephane, eds. *Our Mothers: A Cavalcade in Pictures, Quotation and Description of Late Victorian Women, 1870–1900.* London: Victor Gollancz, 1932.
Branca, Patricia. "Image and Reality: The Myth of the Idle Victorian Woman." In *Clio's Consciousness Raised*, Mary S. Hartman and Lois Banner, eds. New York: Harper & Row, 1974.
———. *Silent Sisterhood: Middle Class Women in the Victorian Home.* London: Croom Helm, 1975.
Branca, Patricia, and Peter N. Stearns. *Modernization of Women in the Nineteenth Century.* The Forum Series. St. Charles, Mo.: Forum Press, 1973.
Briggs, Asa. *Victorian Cities.* 1963. Reprint, New York: Harper Colophon Books, 1970.
Buck, Anne. *Victorian Costume and Costume Accessories.* New York: Thomas Nelson & Sons, 1961.
Burnett, John. *A History of the Cost of Living.* London: Penguin Books, 1969.
Carpenter, Edward. *My Days and Dreams: Being Autobiographical Notes.* London: Allen & Unwin, 1916.
Collins, Leonora, ed. *London in the Nineties.* London: Saturn Press, 1950.

Crossick, Geoffrey. "The Emergence of the Lower Middle Class in Britain: A Discussion." In *The Lower Middle Class in Britain, 1870–1914*, Geoffrey Crossick, ed. New York: St. Martin's Press, 1977.

Crossick, Geoffrey, ed. *The Lower Middle Class in Britain, 1870–1914*. New York: St. Martin's Press, 1977.

Cruse, Amy. *After the Victorians*. 1938. Reprint, London: Allen & Unwin, 1971.

———. *The Victorians and Their Reading*. 1935. Reprint, Boston: Houghton Mifflin, 1962.

Davidoff, Leonore. *The Best Circles: Society Etiquette and the Season*. London: Croom Helm, 1973.

Davidson, Caroline. *A Woman's Work Is Never Done: A History of Housework in the British Isles, 1650–1950*. London: Chatto & Windus, 1982.

Davidson, H. C., ed. *The Book of the Home: A Practical Guide to Household Management*. 8 vols. London: Gresham, 1905.

Dicken's Dictionary of London, 1880: An Unconventional Handbook. London: Charles Dickens, 1880.

Dutton, Ralph. *The Victorian Home: Some Aspects of Nineteenth-Century Taste and Manners*. London: B. T. Batsford, 1954.

DuVall, Nell. *Domestic Technology: A Chronology of Developments*. Boston: G. K. Hall, 1988.

Dyos, H. J., and D. A. Reeder. "Slums and Suburbs." In *The Victorian City: Images and Realities*, vol. 1, H. J. Dyos and Michael Wolff, eds. London: Routledge & Kegan Paul, 1978.

Dyos, H. J., and Michael Wolff, eds. *The Victorian City: Images and Realities*. 2 vols. London: Routledge & Kegan Paul, 1978.

Encyclopedia Britannica, 11th ed. London: Encyclopedia Britannica Co., Ltd., 1911.

Ensor, R.C.K. *England, 1870–1914*. 1936. Reprint, Oxford: Clarendon Press, 1988.

Gay, Peter. *Education of the Senses*. Vol. 1 of *The Bourgeois Experience: Victoria to Freud*. London: Oxford Press, 1984.

Gloag, John. *Victorian Comfort: A Social History of Design from 1830–1900*. London: Adam & Charles Black, 1961.

Gorham, Deborah. *The Victorian Girl and the Feminine Ideal*. Bloomington: Indiana University Press, 1982.

Harrison, J.F.C. *Late Victorian Britain, 1870–1901*. Glasgow: Fontana, 1990.

Harrison, Michael. *The London of Sherlock Holmes*. London: David & Charles Black, 1975.

Harrison, W. Jerome. *The Science of Home Life: A Textbook of Domestic Economy*. London: Thomas Nelson & Sons, 1896.

Hart, Roger. *English Life in the Nineteenth Century*. New York: G. P. Putnam's Sons, 1971.

Hartman, Mary S., and Lois Banner, eds. *Cilio's Consciousness Raised: New Perspectives in the History of Women*. New York: Harper & Row, 1974.

Haskins, C. W. *How to Keep Household Accounts: A Manual of Family Finance*. New York: Harper & Bros., 1902.

Hawks, Ellison. *The Romance of Transport*. New York: Thomas Crowell, 1931.

Hellerstein, Erna Olafson, Leslie Parker Hume, and Karen M. Offen, eds. *Victorian Women: A Documentary Account of Women's Lives in Nineteenth Century England, France, and the United States*. Stanford, Calif.: Stanford University Press, 1981.

Hibbert, Christopher. *The Horizon Book of Daily Life in Victorian England*. New York: American Heritage Publishers, 1975.

Horn, Pamela. *The Rise and Fall of the Victorian Servant*. Dublin: Gill & Macmillan, 1975.

Huggett, Frank E. *Life Below Stairs: Domestic Servants in England from Victorian Times*. London: John Murray, 1977.

Jefferys, James B. *Retail Trading in Britain, 1850–1950*. Cambridge: Cambridge University Press, 1954.

Kanner, Barbara Penny, et al. *Women in Context: Two Hundred Years of British Women Autobiographers, A Reference Guide and Reader*. New York: G. K. Hall, 1997.

Karl Baedeker (Firm). *London and Its Environs: Handbook for Travellers*. Leipsic: Karl Baedeker, 1892.

Langland, Elizabeth. *Nobody's Angels: Middle-Class Women and Domestic Ideology in Victorian Culture*. Ithaca, N.Y.: Cornell University Press, 1995.

Layard, G. S. "Family Budgets: A Lower-Middle-Class Budget." In *Cornhill Magazine* 10 (1901): 656–666.

Lewis, Jane. *Women in England, 1870–1950: Sexual Divisions and Social Change*. Brighton, UK: Wheatsheaf Books, 1984.
Lewis, Roy, and Angus Maude. *The English Middle Classes*. New York: Alfred Knopf, 1950.
Lochhead, Marion. *The Victorian Household*. London: John Murray, 1964.
London *Times*, January 1, 1900.
Macqueen-Pope, W. *Twenty Shillings in the Pound*. London: Hutchinson, 1951.
McBride, Theresa M. " 'As the Twig Is Bent': The Victorian Nanny." In *The Victorian Family: Structure and Stresses*, Anthony S. Wohl, ed. New York: St. Martin's Press, 1978.
———. *The Domestic Revolution: The Modernization of Household Service in England and France, 1820–1920*. New York: Holmes & Meier, 1976.
McLeod, Hugh. *Class and Religion in the Late Victorian City*. London: Croom Helm, 1974.
———. "White Collar Values and the Role of Religion." In *The Lower Middle Class in Britain, 1870–1914*, Geoffrey Crossick, ed. New York: St. Martin's Press, 1977.
Metcalf, Priscilla. *Victorian London*. New York: Praeger, 1972.
Miller, John. " 'Temple and Sewer': Childbirth, Prudery and Victoria Regina." In *The Victorian Family: Structure and Stresses*, Anthony S. Wohl, ed. New York: St. Martin's Press, 1978.
Mitchell, Sally. *Daily Life in Victorian England*. Westport, Conn.: Greenwood, 1996.
Mitchell, Sally, ed. *Victorian Britain: An Encyclopedia*. New York: Garland, 1988.
Morgan, E. Victor. *A History of Money*. Baltimore, Md.: Penguin Books, 1965.
Olsen, Donald J. *The Growth of Victorian London*. New York: Holmes & Meier, 1976.
Panton, Jane. *From Kitchen to Garret: Hints for Young Householders*. 7th ed. London: Ward & Downey, 1890.
Peel, Mrs. C. S. [Dorothy]. *The Labour-Saving House*. London: John Lane, 1917.
Perkin, Joan. *Victorian Women*. London: John Murray, 1993.
Pool, Daniel. *What Jane Austin Ate and Charles Dickens Knew,*

from Hunting to Whist: The Facts of Daily Life in Nineteenth-Century England. New York: Simon & Schuster, 1993.

Robertson, Una A. *The Illustrated History of the Housewife, 1650–1950*. New York: St. Martin's Press, 1997.

Rubinstein, David. "Cycling in the 1890s." In *Victorian Studies* 21 (Autumn 1997): 47–71.

Seaman, L.C.B. *Victorian England: Aspects of English and Imperial History, 1837–1901*. London: Methuen, 1973.

Smith, F. B. *The People's Health, 1830–1910*. New York: Holmes & Meier, 1979.

Spons' Household Manual: A Treasury of Domestic Receipts and Guide for Home Management. London: E. & F. N. Spons, 1887.

Thompson, F.M.L. *The Rise of Respectable Society: A Social History of Victorian Britain, 1830–1900*. Cambridge, Mass.: Harvard University Press, 1988.

———. *Victorian England: The Horse-Drawn Society*. London: University of London Press, 1970.

Turner, E. S. *What the Butler Saw: Two Hundred and Fifty Years of the Servant Problem*. New York: St. Martin's Press, 1963.

Walkley, Christina, and Varda Foster. *Crinolines and Crimping Irons: Victorian Clothes, How They Were Cleaned and Cared For*. London: Peter Owen, 1978.

Ward & Lock's Home Book: A Domestic Encyclopedia. London: Ward, Lock & Co., n.d.

Weightman, Gavin, and Steve Humphries. *The Making of Modern London, 1815–1914*. London: Sidgwick & Jackson, 1983.

White, Cynthia L. *Women's Magazines, 1693–1968*. London: Michael Joseph, 1970.

Wilson, Laura. *Daily Life in a Victorian House*. London: Breslich & Foss, 1993.

Wingfield-Stratford, Esmé. *The Victorian Sunset*. New York: William Morrow, 1932.

Wohl, Anthony S. *Endangered Lives: Public Health in Victorian Britain*. Cambridge, Mass.: Harvard University Press, 1983.

Wohl, Anthony S., ed. *The Victorian Family: Structure and Stresses*. New York: St. Martin's Press, 1978.

OTHER SOURCES, READINGS

Allbutt, Henry Arthur. *Every Mother's Handbook: A Guide to the Management of Her Children from Birth through Infancy and Childhood, with Instructions for Preliminary Treatment of Accidents and Illnesses.* London: Simpton, Marshall, Hamilton, Kent & Co., 1897.

Archer, R. L. *Secondary Education in the Nineteenth Century.* Cambridge: Cambridge University Press, 1921.

Arnstein, Walter L. *Britain Yesterday and Today.* Lexington, Mass.: D. C. Heath, 1983.

———. *The Past Speaks Since 1688: Sources and Problems in British History.* Lexington, Mass.: D. C. Heath, 1981.

Ausubel, Herman. *The Late Victorians: A Short History.* New York: D. Van Nostrand, 1955.

Banks, J. A. *Prosperity and Parenthood: A Study of Family Planning among the Victorian Middle Class.* London: Routledge & Kegan Paul, 1954.

———. "The Way They Lived Then: Anthony Trollope and the 1870s." In *Victorian Studies* 12 (1968): 177–200.

Beeton, Cecil. *The Glass of Fashion.* New York: Doubleday, 1954.

Betjeman, John. *Victorian and Edwardian London from Old Photographs.* New York: Viking, 1969.

Bettman, Otto. *A Pictorial History of Medicine: A Brief Nontechnical Survey of the Healing Arts.* Springfield, Ill.: Charles Thomas, 1956.

Blackwell, Elizabeth. *The Human Element in Sex: Being a Medical Inquiry into the Relation of Sexual Psychology to Christian Morality.* London: J. & A. Churchill, 1894.

Blease, Walter Lyon. *The Emancipation of English Women.* London: David Nutt, 1913.

Bosanquet, Helen. *Social Work in London, 1869–1912: A History of the Charity Organization Society.* London: John Murray, 1914.

Booth, Charles. *Descriptive Map of London Poverty.* 1889. Reprint, London: Topographical Society, 1984.

Bradley, Ian. *The English Middle Classes Are Alive and Kicking.* London: Collins, 1982.

Briggs, Asa. *Victorian Things*. Chicago: University of Chicago Press, 1989.
Browne, Phillis. *Common-sense Housekeeping*. London: Cassell, Petter & Galpin, 1877.
Burnett, John. *Plenty and Want: A Social History of Diet in England from 1815 to the Present Day*. Rev. ed. London: Scholar Press, 1979.
Burstyn, Joan N. *Victorian Education and the Ideal of Womanhood*. London: Croom Helm, 1980.
Cartwright, Frederick F. *A Social History of Medicine*. London: Longmans, 1977.
Cassell's Book of the Household: A Work of References on Domestic Economy. London: British Museum, 1890.
Cline, Cheryl. *Women's Diaries, Journals, and Letters: An Annotated Bibliography*. New York: Garland, 1989.
Clunn, Harold P. *The Face of London*. Rev. ed. London: Phoenix House, 1951.
Collier, Price. *England and the English from an American Point of View*. 1909. Reprint, New York: Charles Scribner's Sons, 1913.
Cook, Chris, and B. Keith, eds. *British Historical Facts, 1830–1900*. London: Macmillan, 1984.
Crow, Duncan. *The Victorian Woman*. London: Allen & Unwin, 1971.
Cullingworth, Charles J. "The Registration of Midwives." In *Contemporary Review* 73 (1898): 394–402.
Cunnington, C. Willett, Phillis Beard, and Charles Beard, eds. *Dictionary of English Costume, 900–1900*. London: Black, 1960.
Davidoff, Leonore. "The Rationalization of Housework." In *Dependence and Exploitation in Work and Marriage*, Diana Barker and Sheila Allen, eds. London: Longmans, 1976.
Davidoff, Leonore, and Catherine Hall. *Family Fortunes: Men and Women of the English Middle Class, 1780–1850*. Chicago: University of Chicago Press, 1987.
DeMarly, Diana. *Fashions for Men: An Illustrated History*. New York: Holmes & Meier, 1985.
Donneson, Jean. *Midwives and Medical Men: A History of Inter-

Professional Rivalries and Women's Rights. London: Heinemann, 1977.

Evans, Joan. *The Victorians.* Cambridge, UK: University Press, 1966.

Fitzgerald, Percy. *The Suburbs.* Vol. 2 of *Victoria's London.* 1893. Reprint of *A Report of London City Suburbs as They Are Today* (London: Ledenhall, 1893), London: Alderman, 1984.

Fraser, Flora, adapter. *Maud: The Diaries of Maud Berkeley.* 1890. Reprint, London: Secher & Warburg, 1985.

Furse, Katherine. *Hearts and Pomegranates: The Story of Forty-Five Years, 1875–1920.* London: Peter Davies, 1940.

Gretton, R. H. *The English Middle Class.* London: G. Bell & Sons, 1917.

Grossmith, George, and Weedon Grossmith. *The Diary of a Nobody.* 1892. Reprint, London: J. M. Dent, 1962.

Habakkuk, H. J. *American and British Technology in the Nineteenth Century: The Search for Labour-Saving Inventions.* Cambridge: Cambridge University Press, 1962.

Haldane, Elizabeth. *From One Century to Another: The Reminiscences of Elizabeth J. Haldane.* London: MacLehose, 1937.

Hamilton, Henry. *England: A History of the Homeland.* New York: W. W. Norton, 1948.

Harrison, Brian. "Women's Health and the Women's Movement in Britain, 1840–1940." In *Biology, Medicine and Society*, Charles Webster, ed. Cambridge: Cambridge University Press, 1981.

Hill, Georgiana. *Women in English Life from Medieval to Modern Times.* 2 vols. London: Richard Bentley & Sons, 1896.

Himes, Norman. *Medical History of Contraception.* New York: Gamut Press, 1963.

Hughes, M. Vivian. *A London Family, 1870–1900.* London: Oxford University Press, 1946.

Lancaster, Bill. *The Department Store: A Social History.* London: Leicester University Press, 1995.

Lasdun, Susan. *Victorians at Home.* New York: Viking, 1981.

Laver, James. *Clothes.* London: Burke, 1952.

Letheby, Henry. *On Food: Its Variety and Chemical Composition.* New York: W. Wood, 1872.

Lilley, Sam. *Men, Machines and History: A Short History of Tools and Machines in Relation to Social Progress.* London: Cobbett Press, 1948.

Markham, Violet R. *Return Passage: The Autobiography of Violet R. Markham.* London: Oxford University Press, 1953.

Martin, Paul. *Victorian Snapshots.* New York: Arno Press, 1973.

Morris, R. J., and Richard Rodger, eds. *The Victorian City: A Reader in British Urban History, 1820–1914.* London: Longmans, 1993.

Murray, Janet Horowitz. *Strong-Minded Women and Other Lost Voices from Nineteenth-Century England.* Harmondsworth, UK: Penguin Books, 1984.

Nelson, Walter Henry. *The Londoners: Life in a Civilized City.* New York: Random House, 1974.

Oliphant, Margaret. *Dress.* London: Macmillan, 1878.

[Panton, Jane.] *Fresh Leaves and Green Pastures.* New York: Brentano's, 1909.

Peel, Mrs. C. S. [Dorothy]. *A Hundred Wonderful Years: Being an Account of Social and Domestic Life in England, 1820–1920.* London: John Lane, 1927.

Perkin, Joan. *Women and Marriage in Nineteenth Century England.* London: Routledge, 1989.

Perry, George, and Nicholas Mason. *The Victorians: A World Built to Last.* New York: Viking, 1974.

Peterson, M. Jeanne. *The Medical Profession in Mid-Victorian London.* Berkeley: University of California Press, 1978.

Rasmussen, Steen Eiler. *London: The Unique City.* London: Pelican Books, 1961.

Raynor, John. *The Middle Class.* London: Longmans, Green, 1969.

Reed, John R. *Victorian Conventions.* Athens: Ohio University Press, 1975.

Routh, H. V. *England Under Victoria.* London, Methuen, 1930.

Sanders, Valerie. *The Private Lives of Victorian Women: Autobiography in Nineteenth-Century England.* New York: St. Martin's Press, 1989.

Sansom, William. *Victorian Life in Photographs.* London: Thames & Hudson, 1974.

Scannel, Dorothy. *Mother Knew Best: Memoir of a London Girlhood.* New York: Pantheon Books, 1975.

Shannon, H. A. "Migration and the Growth of London, 1841–1891: A Statistical Note." In *Economic History Review* 5 (1935): 79–86.
Southern, Richard. *The Victorian Theatre: A Pictorial Survey.* New York: Theatre Arts Books, 1970.
Stanley, Liz, ed. *The Dairies of Hannah Cullwick, Victorian Maidservant.* Reprint, New Brunswick, N.J.: Rutgers University Press, 1989.
Stoddart, Anna M. *Life and Letters of Hannah Pipe.* Edinburgh: William Blackwood & Sons, 1908.
Swan, Annie S. *Courtship and Marriage and the Gentle Art of Homemaking.* London: Hutchinson, 1894.
Thomson, David. *England in the Nineteenth Century: 1815–1914.* 1950. London: Penguin Books, 1983.
Trager, James, ed. *The People's Chronology: A Year-by-Year Record of Human Events from Prehistory to the Present.* New York: Holt, Rinehart & Winston, 1979.
Tucker, Herbert F., ed. *A Companion to Victorian Literature and Culture.* London: Blackwell, 1999.
Ulrich, Laurel Thatcher. *Good Wives: Image and Reality in the Lives of Women in Northern New England, 1650–1750.* New York: Knopf, 1982.
Vicinus, Martha, ed. *Suffer and Be Still: Women in the Victorian Age.* Bloomington: Indiana University Press, 1972.
———. *A Widening Sphere: Changing Roles of Victorian Women.* Bloomington: Indiana University Press, 1977.
Warren, Mary Anne. *The Nature of Women: An Encyclopedia and Guide to the Literature.* Inverness, Calif.: Edgepress, 1980.
Webb, Beatrice. *My Apprenticeship.* 1926. In conjunction with the London School of Economics and Political Science. Reprint, Cambridge: Cambridge University Press, 1979.

Index

"Accomplishments" for middle-class girls, 8, 124
Account recording, 81–82
Acton, William, 96, 104 n.2
Administrators, suburbs for, 22
Advertising: as "puffery," 160; use as hiring domestics in newspapers, 72; use of brand names in magazine, 166
Aereated Bread Company (A.B.C.) tea shops, 154
Air pollution, 19–21
Albert Hall, 154, 173
Alhambra theatre, motion picture at, 137, 175
Allbutt, Henry: advice on contraception by, 100; advice on pregnancy by, 101; description of doctors' actions during the child delivery process by, 103

Appearance, physical, of MCMW, difficulty in determining, 35
Army and Navy Stores, 163
Artificial Feeding of Infants. *See* Bottle-feeding
Artists, suburbs for, 22
"The Art of Cookery," food preparation, English style, 60–61
Automobiles, 174

Bainbridge department store, 162–63; initiator of establishing variety of departments under one roof, 162
"The Bazaar," 162
Beeton, Isabella, opinions on: advantages of sewing machine, 67; breast-feeding as health hazard for mothers,

116 n.16; importance of fashion, 42
Beeton, Isabella, advice on: beauty enhancers, 36; choosing a house, 27; "digestive time table," 62; dinner party giving, 134, 135; importance of leisure activities, 149; keeping household account book, 81–82; luncheon content, 64–65; need for "professed cook" for formal dining, 77; preparation of "good plain dinners," 61; vegetable cooking time, 62; wallpaper selection, 30
Berlin, electric trams in, 173, 180
Benjamin Hyam & Company, 164
Bicycle, 174–75; cost of, 153; use by older middle-class matron, 152–53; use by younger middle-class women, 153, 185, 188; use of in business, 175; widespread use of, 174–75
Birmingham, cable-hauled trams in, 173
Birth control methods and devices, 99–100; abortifacient pills, 99; abortion, 99; abstinence, 99; advertisements of, 100; availability of information about, 98; *coitus interruptus*, 99; the condom, 99–100; female contraceptives, descriptions of, 100; the "safe period" for nonconception, 99; spread of knowledge of, 100
Birth rate drop, 1875–1900, 98–99; desire for rising standard of living in, 98; medical concern for female health as factor in, 98–99; multiple causation of, 98; publication of birth control information in, 98
Bissell, Melville, 49
Blackwell, Elizabeth, 96
Boarding schools for girls: "accomplishments" teaching in, 124; cost of, 7, 124
Board schools, 123. *See also* Education, boys: alternatives for parents in choosing
Book of Household Management Management [and] a Guide to Cookery in all Branches (Isabella Mary Beeton), 33 n.12; as cookbook, 61; persistent upper-class orientation of, 139 n.23; social ritual of dinner, 63. *See also* Beeton, Isabella, advice on; Beeton, Isabella, opinions on
Books, cost of, 151; children's, 112; cost of subscriptions for borrowing, 151; serialization in magazines of, 151. *See also* Leisure activities, personal: book reading as
Boot and shoe industry, changes in, 161
Booth, Cecil, 49
Booth, Charles, 141
Bottle-feeding: 110–11; dan-

gers to infant of, 110; doctor-inducted guilt in mothers for, 111. *See also* Breast-feeding

Boxing Day, 130

Breast-feeding: as against bottle-feeding, controversy about, 110–11; dangers to mothers of, 116 n.16; doctors' insistence on, 110–11; mothers' distaste for, 110. *See also* Bottle-feeding

Brighton, electric street lights in, 173

Bristol, electric street lights in, 173

British Mother's Magazine, 101

Brixton, 22

Brussels, electric trams in, 173

Buckingham Palace, 16

Budget: imbalance problems of, 93; domestic manuals' omission of husband's role in devising, 84; suggested guidelines for, 84

Budgeting of expenditures: *ad hoc* categories used by housewife in, 90–93; "catch-all" category in, 90, 91–92; changes over twenty-five years in, 85; comparison of methods used by men and women in, 89; difficulty in, 92–93; encumbered items in, 91; food expenditures allowed by housewife-as-cook in, 60; known and flexible category in, 90, 91; known and inflexible category in, 90–91

Budget comparisons, 1874 and 1901: charitable contributions, 87–88; food costs, 87; clothing allocations, 87; cost of servants' wages, 87; cost of vacations, 88; education allowances, 88; housing costs, 87; life and fire insurance allowance, 87; living amenities allowance, 88; medical costs for children, 88; recreation expenses, 88; religious participation costs, 87–88

Budget samples, for 1874 and 1901, 84–86

Builders and developers, expansion of suburbs by, 21

Bull, Thomas, 101

Buses, electrically powered. *See* London, 1900

Camberwell, 22

Carpet sweeper, mechanical, 49

Carriage, petroleum-propelled. *See* London, 1900

Carriages, horseless, anticipation in promise of, 188

Cars, steam-powered. *See* London, 1900

"Cash-on-purchase" policy, department stores: advantage to retailer of, 164; attraction of housewife to, 164; effect on housewife's money management of, 83; modification by

Harrods of, 164. *See also* Department store innovations
Census statistics: drop in birth rate in, 98; lack of class-specific data in, 11 n.12; lack of income/occupation correlation data in, 5; marriage age of middle-class women in, 4; shortage of governesses in, 7, 12 n.24
Change: housewife as engine for, xiii–xiv, 186–89; housewife's lack of program for, 189; nontraditional stance by traditional housewife for, 189
Change, factors in housewife's support of: acknowledged weight of servants' complaints, 87; discovered advantages of improved domestic technology, 188; perception of consequences of medical profession's resistance to change, 188–89; recognition of need for household drudgery relief, 186–87; recognition of need for improved technology in clothing matters, 188; recognition of opening horizons in new mobility technology, 188
Chaperonage, 185
Chaperones, 8
"A Character," servants' references, value of, 73
Charing Cross, 16
"Charing Cross Kitchener," 182

Charitable activities, suburban: 145–46; change in reasons for middle-class, 145; diminishing housewife interest in, 146; nonleadership role of housewife in, 146; unclear association of religious institutions with, 144; wealthy class's participation in, 144–45
Charity's ritual visits, 130
Charles Bradlaugh–Annie Besant trial, 98
Chemist as patent medicine source, 109, 114. *See also* Disease, childood, patent medicines as relief in
"Childbed fever." *See* Puerperal Fever
Childbirth: description of, 103–4; doctors role in health hazard of, 103–4; fear of, 97; health hazard to mothers of, 109; maternal mortality rate during, 97; underreporting of deaths at, 109–10
Childbirth, imminent: lack of data on mother's preference for doctor against midwife at, 102; presumptions of doctor's enlightened help during, 102
Child care, direct role of mother in, 76, 119, 121; later elimination of maternal duties of, 185; new attitude regarding role of unabated crying, harsh discipline in, 121; preference for nurse-

Index

maid in, 120; unclear role of spouse in, 121–22; use by housewife of own mother, older sister to help with, 119; use of servants to help in, 119

Children, adult, social activities and work of, 185

Children, older: organized activities for, 129; seashore activities of, mother-arranged, 133

Children, young: anticipation of summer holidays by, 132; religious practices of, 142; seashore activities of, 133

Chloroform, 102, 103–4

Chocolate, eating, manufacture of, 161

The Christmas Holiday, 130

Church, suburban: nonreligious aspect of attendance at, 142, 143; role for family of, 142; social activities for adults in, 142–43; social activities for children in, 142–43

Cigarettes, manufacture of, 161

Circle line, 16

Civil servants, suburbs for, 22

Civil service, job opportunities for young women in, 155

Clerks, retail sales: jobs for young women as, 155, 176

Clerks: suburbs for higher paid, 22; suburbs for lower-middle-class, 22

Clothes, women's: coats, 40; costume accessories, 40–41; dress descriptions, 38–40; dressmakers role in, 38, 67–68; fashion styles of, 38; shoes, 41; undergarments, 40

Clothing: construction of, 38; corsets as element in, 40; difficulty to generalize about, 37; fabrics, natural, of, 38; housewife's responsibility for family, 66; husband's purchase of own, 66; return of the bustle in, 37–38, 39; return of the crinoline and "crinolette," in 37; seasonal changes and fashions of, 37; storage for, 54; use of sewing machine in construction of, 38

Clothing, summer seasonal review of, 132

Club for women: role of department store as, 165

Cologne, electric trams in, 173

"Comfort stations," lack of, 154

Communications, technological modernization of, 175

Commuters into London, 16

Complexion beautifiers, names of, 37

Condoms, use of, 97, 99–100. *See also* Birth control methods and devices; Contraception

Conquest, John, 101

Consumer goods: delayed industrial revolution in manufacture of, 161; introduction of new, 101; production in

anticipation of demand for, 161–62
"Consumerism" of middle-class housewife: department-store response to, 82, 162–67; rise of nineteenth-century, 159–67. *See also* Department store innovations
Contraception, bride's limited knowledge of, 96–97; devices for, 96, 99–100; reliance on mechanical means of, 99; differences of views on, 105 n.16. *See also* Birth control methods and devices
Cook, employed: difficulties of hiring of, 77–78; difficulties of firing, 78; disadvantageous position of housewife with regard to, 78; friction between housewife and, 77–78; improved working conditions as aid in hiring of, 184; limited skills for food preparation of, 63; multiple tasks involved in being, 59–60; perquisites demanded by, 78; wages of, 59, 77
Cook, plain, qualifications of, 77
Cook, professed: lack of training schools for, 63–64, 77; probable absence in moderate-income household, 77; qualifications of, 77
Cook, Thomas, 137
Cooking range, coal-burning, 60
Cook's Tours: cultural activities on, 138; cost of, 138; group trip of British Isles, 137; overseas trips, 138, 180
Co-operative Societies stores, 163
Cornhill Magazine (1901), sample budget for family in, 85–86
Cosmetic aids, advice on names of, uses of, 36–37
Crystal Palace, 3, 154, 171
Customer amenities. *See* Department store innovations
"The customer is always right," 165

Daimler, Gottfried, 174
Dalston, 22
Decibel level of traffic, lack of knowledge about, 19
Dental care for children, 114
Department store innovations: attention to housewife's opinions, 166; attractive display of goods in store, 82; attractive window displays, 162; "cash on purchase," policy, 164; comparatively low prices, 82, 163; consumer-friendly attitude, 164–65; customer amenities, 82; customer conveniences, 165; customer services, 162; many departments under one roof, 162, 163; multiplicity of goods, large range of selections, 82, 163; openly displayed goods, 164; openly displayed prices on goods,

162; the periodic sale, 162; prepackaged brand name goods, 166; quick guaranteed delivery of goods, 164; "satisfaction guaranteed," 164

Department stores: as an "alternative environment," 165; early examples of, 162, 163; evolution of, 163; influence on housewife money-management role, 82; innovative leadership in, 162; new selling policies of, 82–83; response to housewife's "consumerism," 162–66; selling methods of, 162; shift from low-price policy to "amenities" stress by, 164

Diaphragm, rubber, 100

Dickens's Dictionary of London, 154

Dickins & Jones, 163

Diet as element in health, 108

Dinner: middle-class rituals of, 66, 135; preparation by housewife of, 65–66; styles of serving dinner, 135, 136; upper-class rituals of, 65–66

Dinner in the city, couples activity, 137

Diesel, Rudolph, 174

Diphtheria, 113. *See also* Disease, childhood

Disease, childhood: advice by domestic manuals on ailments and, 113; diphtheria, incidence of, 113; disinterest by medical profession in, 113; inadequacy of medical knowledge regarding, 112; measles, incidence of, 113; patent medicines as relief in, 114; rejection by mothers of death as inevitability in, 112; scarlet fever, description and fatal incidence of, 112–13; small pox as disfiguring but not fatal illness as, 113

Distributive trades, mid-century changes in, 161

District line, 16

Doctors. *See* Medical profession

Doctors, suburbs for, 22

Domestic manuals: advice on child care and education, 119, 121; advice on prompt bill payment, 82; advice on rental housing deficiencies, 28, beauty hints and enhancers, 36–37; budgeting discussions, 84; cautions regarding marketing deceptions practiced by cooks, 61; cautions regarding servants' character reference forgeries, 73; childhood diseases information, 113; dressmaking advice, 67; etiquette of food service, 63. *See also entries under specific names*

Dresses, women. *See* Clothes, women's; Clothing

Dressmakers. *See* Clothes, women's

Dress patterns, 67

Dress reform, middle-class matron's disinterest in, 42

Drinking habits as factor in health, 108
Dry-cleaning of clothing: commercial fluids available for, 55; common compounds used in, 55, 57 n.30
Dunlap, J. D., 153

Economics as root of "The Servant Problem," 79
Economy, healthy, municipal pollution seen as sign of, 20
Edinburgh, cable trams in, 173
Education, boys: allowance in women's budget for, 92; alternatives for parents in choosing, 123–24; cost of, 92, 124; limited role by mother in, 123; long duration as element in increased cost of, 88; omission in men's budgets to provide for, 88; schools preferred by middle class for, 124
Education, girls: "accomplishments," as boarding school teaching in, 124; alternatives available for, 124, 125; change of mother's attitude regarding training for paid work, 125; maternal role in, 124; housekeeping arts as part of, 7; home schooling as part of, 7; nonuse of governesses in, 7; presence of boys in family as limiting, 6; self-taught element in, 8; training in higher professions judged unnecessary in, 126; unbudgeted expense of, 88
Educational Act of 1879, 123
Electric appliances, 183
Electric lamps, incandescent, invention of, 173
Electric lighting in business and commerce, 173
Electric power, domestic, high cost of, 182–83
Electric street lighting, early experimental display of, 16, 173
Empire theatre, motion pictures at, 137, 175
Employment, paid, new opportunities for young women in, 125, 155; kinds of jobs offered as, 155; usefulness of experience of, 125
Employment agencies, 72–73
Engine for change, the MCMW as inadvertent, xiii–xiv; 186–89
Englishwoman's Domestic Magazine, discouragement of religious submissions by, 143
Environmental factors as element of health, 108
Euston, 16
Eye care, schools' role in providing boy's, 114–15

Family, extended, absence of data about middle-class, 155 n.2
Family health. *See* Disease, childhood; Illnesses, adult; Illnesses, women

Family limitation, relation of cost of education to, 88
Family size, 6, 96, 98
Fashion: cost as factor of, 41; influence of upbringing on views of, 42; influence on woman's time and family money of styles and, 38–39; matron's mixed views of high, 41–42; variations to clothing to accommodate, 41
Father, role of, in child care, 121–22
Finances. *See* Money management by housewife; Money management by spouse
Fireplaces, as heat provider, 28; soot as element in chimney air pollution from, 19; venting flues in, 28; work involved in cleaning, 48, 120, 183. *See also* Household tasks of servant
First aid, suggestions in domestic manuals on, 114
Food allowance, keeping an account book for, 81–82
Food choices: categories suggested by experts for, 62; cost as criterion for, 63; guidelines offered for, 62; housewife's cooking ability as determining, 63; husband's preferences as setting, 63
Food diet, inclusion of seasonal fruits and vegetables as possibly contributing to healthful, 62–63

Food industries, changes in, 161
Food preparation, daily: 63–66; breakfast content, 64; breakfast tasks of housewife and servant, 48; luncheon service and, 49; prior work in kitchen before dinner, 50; routine followed in home for, 64–66; tea service and, 49–50
Food preservation, 54
Food refrigeration, absence of, 183
Foodstuffs: cost of, 59–60; influx from abroad of, 162
Food trade outlets, experimentation in, 162
Forest Hill, 22
Fortnum & Mason, 129, 163
Frankfurt, electric trams in, 173
Free Public Library and Reading Room, 151
French recipes and menus, Mrs. Beeton's reproduction of, 61
Fruits of Philosophy, reissue of, 98
Fully detached house, 27
Functions of Middle-class Married Woman (MCMW): viii–ix; as clothes manager, 66–68; as child caregiver, 119–23; as cook/marketer/meal planner, 59–66; as employer, 71–79; as education manager for her girls, 124–26; as financial manager, 81–

93; as health guardian, 107–115; as housecleaner, 47–52; as laundress, 52–55; as religious and charities arbiter, 141–49; as shopper, 159–167; as social activities coordinator, 129–38

Furnishings: accumulation of, 32; amount and variety of, 32; change in, 181, 182; description of, 182

Furniture: attractions for young couple of massive, 30; description of, 30–31; difficulty of cleaning, 52; functional nature of servant's, 32; hire-purchase plan used for replacing, 92; joint venture by couple in choosing, 30; pattern books as means of choosing, 30–31; suites as mode of buying, 30; unattractive appraisal by moderns of Victorian, 30

Games and activities: of childhood, 122; mother-provided lullabies, 122

Gas appliances, preference for, 182

Gas, Light & Coke Company, 182

Gas lighting in home, 28; absence in bedrooms of, 52

Gas space heaters, 183

Gas supplies: privately owned companies' control of, 177

General Electric Company, 183

General Post Office (GPO), 16–17

General servant. *See* Servant, general

Genetics as factor in state of health, 108

George Hitchcock (department store), 163

Germany: mentioned in London *Times* article, 172; use of electric trolley in, 173

Girl, young: birthplace of, 5, 6; charity, church work of, 8; coming-out ceremony for, 9; cooking and housecleaning responsibilities of, 7–8; duties to family members of, 8, 13 n.30; early education of, 6–7; impermissibility of paid work for, 9; maternal control over social activities of, 10; nonutility of "accomplishments" for, 8; place in large family of, 6; schooling of, 6; training in household arts of, 7; upbringing of, 6

Girl's Friendly Society, 72

Girls Public Day School Company and High Schools, 88, 125

Governess: education of preschool boys by, 123; unlikelihood of girl in moderate-income family having, 7, 125; wages of, 12 n.24, 125

Gramophone, 175

Greater London, 15, 16

Great Exhibition of 1851, 3, 15
Great Fog of 1886, 20
Gynecology, development in nineteenth century of, 101

Hackney, 22
Hackney cabs, 17–18
Hair, advice on care and treatment of, 36
Hammersmith, 22
Hampstead, 22
Hangers, clothes, absence of, 54–55
Hansom cabs, 17–18
Harrods, 129, 163
Health, children: birthright of well-being expected in, 112; feelings of helplessness, lack of control over, 107, 108, 111, 112
Health: environmental factors affecting, 108; general helplessness in concerns about, 108; hard data lacking on couple's premarital, 108; housewife's early postmarital, 108; personal habits as factor in, 108; state of husband's health, 25, 108; shift by matron to concerns about adult, 185
Heaters, gas, 182
Help, temporary: laundry day washerwoman as, 53; seasonal tasks require hiring of, 51
Hints to Mothers . . . during the Period of Pregnancy . . . , 101

Hiring registries, 72–73
Holburn, experimental electric street lights in, 23 n.13
Holiday abroad, housewife's activities during, 138
Holiday by the sea. *See* Seashore holiday
Horse droppings: amount of, 18; disposal of, 18–19; smell of, 19
Horticultural Society, 154
House, 1875: description and location of rooms in, 31–32; awkward shape as complicating cleaning of, 51; coal-burning stove as owner-provided equipment in, 60; coal-burning stove as source of heat in, 60; external features of standard, 27; lack of flushing toilet in, 32; lack of separate room for bath and sink in, 31–32; layout of, 29–30; reasons for original defects in, 28–29; rental as standard in, 26; stairs in, 29, 30; standard layout in, 29; storerooms in, 30; unavailability of range-attached hot-water boiler in, 60; unfurnished state as standard in, 30
House, 1900: baths in separate rooms in, 181; gas lighting in, 181; gas range in, 60, 182; ground-floor location of kitchen in, 181; improved layout of, 181; innovative schemes for adding more

baths in, 181; installation of commodity lift in, 181; stoves for heating as replacement of fireplaces in, 183

Housecleaning: activities involved in, 47–50; air pollution residue ("the blacks") complicating, 20; lighting as problem in, 51–52; piped water inadequacies as complication in, 52; special problems in house's public rooms for, 48

Household tasks of housewife: continuation during pregnancy of, 103; cooking/ marketing and clothes management as preferred, 59; dealing with food venders as one of, 49; domestic manual listings as too demanding, 47 enumeration of, 48–51; early familiarity with work aspects of, 47; mending on sewing machine as one of, 49; physical work involved in, 47; shopping for perishables as one of, 49. *See also* Household tasks of servant

Household tasks of servant: 48– 50; kitchen cleanup, 50, 60; periodic cleaning, 50; seasonal cleaning, 50–51; special pre-Sabbath attention to, 50

House-hunting: activity of couple in, 26; advice on choosing house during, 27–28; cost as factor in husband's participation in, 26; deficiencies encountered while, 27–29; desirable location a factor in choosing house in, 27; layout of only minor concern in, 27; structure of home a consideration in, 27; wife's concerns in, 26

The Housewife, 150

Housewife, later years: acquisition of cook, 184; acquisition of second housemaid, 184; employer role exercised in more relaxed fashion by 185; lack of data regarding financial management by, 185; lightening of domestic routines, 184; limited role as coordinator of daughters' activities, 185–86; user of advanced technology in clothes management, 188

Housing: architectural style as factor in cost of, 27; availability of affordable, 22, 27; minimum amenities provided by owner in, 27–28; rise overtime in cost of, 87, 181; size as factor in cost of, 27

Howe, Elias, 66

Husband of MCMW. *See* Spouse of MCMW

"Ice safe," storing of perishables in, 61

Idleness of young girls (mid-1800s), 12 n.29

Illnesses, adult: description of, 115; doctor's advice solicited for catastrophic, 108; incidence of cancer as, 115; onset of physical or mental, 180; reluctance to call doctor for ordinary, 108–9; use of patent medicine for, 109, 114

Illnesses, children. *See* Disease, childhood

Illnesses, infants. *See* Infant mortality

Illnesses, women: high incidence of death from tuberculosis among, 35, 109; incidence of respiratory, 109. *See also* Puerperal fever

Income/occupation correlation, lack of official data on, 4; validity of Baxter's *National Income* (1868) on, 5, 11 n.13; validity of Colquhoun's *Treatise on Indigence* (1803) on, 11 n.13

Infant mortality: convulsions as major cause of, 114; cow's milk as contributing to high incidence of, 111; diarrhea as factor in, 111; doctor's refusal to accept any responsibility for, 110–11; high incidence of, 110

Infections of childhood, helplessness of both doctors and mothers to cure, 114

Insurance, fire and life, 87, 91

Internal combustion engine automobiles, absence in London of, 174

Irons, clothes: electric and coal-heated, 54; mangle, 54

Jenner, Edward, 113

Kendal, Milne & Faulkner department store ("The Bazaar"): innovations (attractive window supplies, open prices on all goods and periodic sale) initiated by, 162

Kennington, 22

Kensington, 22

Kerosene (paraffin) lamps, 56 n.12

Kew Gardens, 154

King's Cross, 16

Kitchen as workplace, 60; later installation of gas stove in, 182

Kitchen gadgets and tools, stocking of, department-store response to housewife's wishes in, 166

Knowlton, Charles, 98

The Labour-Saving House, 187–88

The Ladies Home Journal, 150

Lamps, kerosene or oil: source of artificial light, 28; trimming and cleaning chore of, 48, 52

Laundresses, 53

Laundry: allocation of jobs in doing, 55; amount of, 53; hand scrubbing of, 53; harshness of bleaches, soaps used for, 53; list of items included in, 53; other equipment used, 53–54; periodic (not weekly) occurrence of,

53; physical labor involved in doing, 55; use of ceiling raised drying racks, 54; water heating requirements for, 53
Lawn tennis, 10, 153
Lawson, H. J., 153
Lawyers, suburbs for, 22
Layard, G. S., 86
Leisure activities, couple: card playing as, 153; a variety of sports as, 153
Leisure activities, personal: attending cultural events with friends as, 153–54; book reading as, 151–52; difficulties in London and suburbs for unescorted women engaged in, 154; doing charitable works as, 152, gradual involvement in, 150; "grandmothering" as possible, 152; impossibility of paid employment for matron as, 155; magazine reading as, 150–52; refusal of bride to engage in, 149–50; shopping as, 159–67; visiting friends as, 152; visiting parents or siblings as, 150
Letters to a Mother . . . Embracing the Subjects of Pregnancy, Childbirth [and] *Nursing*, 101
Libraries, free public, 7; inability of London to develop system of, 177
Libraries, private: Mudie's and W. H. Smith as popular lending, 151; for nonfiction, serious literature, 151; religious society, 7
Life expectancy, statistics on, 115
Lighting in home, 52; inadequacy of early owner-provided gas as, 28
Lip makeup, creation and use of, 36–37
Liverpool, electric street lights in, 173
London, 1875: absence of municipally provided water in, 29; air pollution in, 19–21; area size of, 15; boroughs, counties and cities of Greater, 15, 23 n.2; gas street lights of, 16; horse droppings on streets of, 18; mail delivery in, 17; modern city features of, 16; "pea-souper" fogs of, 19–20; people-carrying conveyances of, 17–18; plumbing in houses of, 16; population of, 15; postal districts in, 17; public health hazards of, 108; public omnibuses in, 16; railway commuters entering, 16; railway stations in, 16; sanitary improvement legislation of, 16; sewage drainage of, 16; street cleanup problems in, 19; street traffic volume of, 17; telegraph in, 16–17; traffic noise in, 19; trams in, 16; tourist attractions of, 15–16; trash collection in, 16; underground railways of, 16

London, 1900: democratic representation in, 176; lack of electric street lighting in, 173; lack of electric trams in, 173; lag in local reform of, 176; late appearance of internal combustion omnibuses in, 174; petroleum-propelled carriages in, 174; population of, 172; presence of horse-drawn conveyances in, 173; presence of private water monopolies, 176–77; reluctance to change in, 173–74; steam- and electric-powered vehicles in, 174; street and thoroughfare improvements in, 173; tourist attractions of, 172–73; traffic congestion in, 173
London, City of, 15, 16
Londoners, attitude toward municipal pollution, 20; movement to suburbs by, 21
London General Omnibus Company, 16
London Maternal Association, 101
London, Past and Present, 16
London *Times*, Jan. 1, 1900 issue of the, 171–72
Low Countries, use of electric trolleys in, 173
Lower-middle class clerks, suburbs for, 22
Luxuries in department stores, housewife's response to, 166

Madame Tussaud's waxworks, 129

Magazines, domestic: articles of interest in, 150; availability of, 150; indifference to religion in, 143–44
Maid-of-all-work. *See* Servant, general
Mail delivery. *See* London, 1875
Management of expenditures by housewife, 82
Management of finances, 81–93
Management of servants, 71, 73–77, 79
Managerial people, suburbs for, 22
Manual of Domestic Economy, sample budget in, 84–85
Margarine, manufacture of, 161
Marketing for food: bulk purchasing as means of saving money in, 62; cooking job as including, 59; domestic manuals as source of information about, 61; initial inexperience in, 61; preference by housewife as compared to other tasks for, 61; vendor home delivery in lieu of, 62
Market forces, significant changes in, 161
Marriage (mid-1800s): activities permitted young girl as she approached, 9; age of middle-class men at, 4; description of ceremony of, 10; role of father after proposal of, 10; successful efforts by mother

in guiding, 9–10; suitor's presentation of proposal of, 10; wedding trip, 10
Marriage, first year: bride's ignorance of sexual aspects of, 95–96; decisions by couple regarding family size in, 97; discovery by bride of sexual pleasure in, 96, 105 n.26
Marshall, Albert T., 56 n.6
Marylebone, 16
Mass production of consumer goods, start of, 161
Matrimonial prospects, daughters (1890s), matron's limited options in channeling, 185
Maytag, Frederick, 54
MCMW. *See* Housewife, later years; middle-class housewife; mistress of the house; motherhood
Measles. *See* Diseases, childhood
Medical knowledge of female problems, meager extent among general practitioners of, 102
Medical profession: advances in female-problem surgery of, 102; blame for infant mortality placed on mothers by, 110–11; cost of adult house call by, 108–9; dangers posed to pregnant women by, 102; dangers posed to family by conservatism of, 107–8; lack of instruction to mothers on safe bottle-feeding by, 111; lack of interest in family health problems by, 107; reluctance to use chloroform at childbirth by, 102, 103–4; resistance to change by, 107–8
Men's clothing industry, changes in, 161
Menu planning as part of cooking job, 59
Metropolitan Association for Befriending Young Servants, 72
Metropolitan line, 16
Middle class: definition of, 4; movement toward London of, 6; occupations comprising, 4–5; occupations in market towns for, 6; occupations in villages for, 5–6
Middle-class girls (mid-1800) and servants' work, 7–8
Middle-class housewife as "representative figure, disrupting factors to, 180
Midwives at childbirth, 102
Mistress of the house, housewife's authority as, 47
Modernization, process of, 189
Money, Victorian, explanation of, 191–92
Money management by housewife: ambiguous check writing power in, 83, 93 n.11; ambiguous responsibility for paying of bills, 93 n.6; anxieties inherent in, 81; earlier limited responsibility for, 81, 82; housewife's indifference

to "hands-on" manager role in, 89; ignorance of husband's income as part of problem of, 89–90; indirect, covert approach to, 89; lack of data on cash-handling in, 83; payment of servants' wages as part of, 91; unanswered questions regarding, 83

Money management by spouse: as part of overseas holiday arrangements, 138; voice in, 82

Mortality rate, maternal, 109–10

Motherhood, bride's feelings towards, 96–97

"Mothering" as innate function of all women, 119

The Mother's Companion, 150

The Mother's Friend, 101

Mother-to-be, daily activities of, 103

Motor car, contribution to improved quality of life by, 19; late arrival of internal combustion engine, 174; protests against, 174

Mudie's bookstore, 151

Municipal pollution, 19–21

Music hall entertainment, 137

Nanny: description and training of, 119–20, 121; high wages as factor in nonuse of, 120; housewife's hiring objection of, 76, 119; housewife's objection to mother-substitute role of, 120; warnings to mother of dangers in use of, 120

National Gallery 16, 154

National Income, reliability acknowledged, 11 n.13

"The National" of Thomas Twyford, 32

National Gallery, 16, 154

National Portrait Gallery, 154

National Sunday League, 142

The Nelson column, 16

New Cross, 22

Newspapers and magazines, rise in cost of, 88

Nurse, monthly, 104

Nursemaid: child-related duties of, 120; mother's role (mid-1800s) as, 6; nonchild-related duties of, 6, 76, 120; older sister's role as, 6; preference of mother for child care of, 76; preferred second servant as, 75–76; recruitment and training of, 76; similarities to general servant of, 76; tenure of, 76–77; wages of, 76

Nursery, home: physical aspects of, 121; unisex nature of education in, 122

Obstetrics, nineteenth-century development of, 101–2

Occupation/income correlation. *See* Income/occupation correlation

Old age, onset of, 115. *See also*

Illnesses, adult, description, onset of physical or mental
Omnibuses, 16, 174
Opiates in medicines, 114
"Outer ring," portion of counties comprising Greater London's, 15

Paddington, 16, 22
Paid work, impermissibility of middle-class women doing, 9
Pantomines, 130
Paris, horseless carriages in, 180
Parliament, Houses of, 15
Patent medicines: aid for adult illness of, 109; health hazards to children of, 114; manufacture of new, 161; use by mothers of treating childhood ailments with, 114
Patronage, greater, response by housewife to department store attitude through, 166
"Peasouper," 19–20
Pediatrics, absence of science of, 113
Periodic household tasks, 50
Personal fulfillment activities. *See* Leisure activities, personal
Peter Robinson (department store), 163
Phaeton, steam-driven, 174
Philanthropic activity. *See* Charitable activities, suburban
Phonograph, 175
Pimlico, 22

Plumbing, domestic: quality provided by owner of, 27–28; reasons for delay in proper installation of, 183–84
Pollution, air, 19–21
Postal districts, London, 17
Prayers, family, disappearance of daily, 141
Pregnancy: advice in books, magazines articles on, 101; bedrest during, 103; continued housework during, 103; lack of constructive advice on, 101; limited knowledge of doctors about, 101–2; matron's recollection of own mother's, 96; medical support for spacing in, 98; prevention of, 97; probability of early, 97; reaction to illness of, 100–101; reluctance to call doctor during, 103; restriction of activities during, 100; seclusion ("confinement") during, 103; symptoms of, 100; thoughts on, 96
Prenatal care, mother-to-be, 101
Preschool child: games of, 122–23; limited supervision of, 122, 123; limited rigorous schooling of, 123; moral instruction of, 123
Prices and cash flow, retailing policies relating to, 162
Professional people, suburbs for, 22
Proprietors, inventive, 162

Public Health Act of 1875, 23 n.10
Public health hazards, decrease of, 108
Puerperal fever: doctors' delay in taking measures to prevent, 109; doctors' roles in transmission of, 102, 109; high incidence among middle class of, 109; high mortality rates of, 109; underreporting of deaths due to, 109–10
Punch and Judy shows, 133

Railway stations, 16. *See also* London (1875), railway stations
"Rationalization" of housework, 184
Reading clubs, 152
Ready-made clothes: department store response to "consumerism," 166; end of housewife as seamstress due to appearance of, 184–85; initial introduction of, 66
Recipes: domestic manuals, women's magazines as sources of, 61
Recreation: cost of, 88, 90, 91–92; religious sects engagement in secular, 136
Red Flag Act, 174
Refreshment room, 162. *See also* Whiteley's Department Store
Refrigeration, home: lack of, 49

Relationship, symbiotic, between MCMW and department store, 167
Religion: attendance of family at Sunday services, 143; decline in commitment within family to, 142; diminution of matron's personal commitment to, 143; diminution of matron's religious role in home, 143; limited data on home participation of late-century middle-class family in, 141, 144; matron's, spouse's roles in family practice of, 142; possible divergence from earlier practices of, 144; rising cost of participation in institutions of, 87–88; spouse's community role in suburban, 144
Remington, E., 175–76
Remington Typewriter Company, 176
Retail shop, traditional (mid-1800s): absence of consumer-friendliness by owner of, 160–61; assumption of high business acuity by owner of, 161; high prices in, 161; limited stock selection in, 161; possibly shoddy goods at, 161; selling methods of, 160; size of, 160
"Retiring rooms," 162
Roller skating, 10, 153
"The Rover," 153
Royal Albert Hall, 154, 173
Royal Opera House, 16

St. James Hall, 154
St. John's Wood, 22
St. Pancras, 16
St. Paul's Cathedral, 16
Scarlet fever. *See* Disease, childhood
Schools, boys. *See* Education, boys
Scotland, electric buses in, 174
Scrubbing boards. *See* Laundry
Seamstress, role of housewife as, 66–68; end to matron's role as, 184
Seashore holiday: choosing the resort town for, 131; as organized family activity, 130–33; part-time attendance by husband on, 131; preparation for departure for, 131–32; possible joint tenancy with another family at, 131; unpacking at home after, 133
Seasonal tasks, house, 50–51; review of clothing for summer holiday as, 132; special home care arrangements while at seashore resort as, 132
Secretarial schools, 185
Semi-detached houses, 27
Sermon, Sunday, 143
Servant, general: complaints by housewife of lack of quality of, 72; decreased size of hiring pool for, 72; development of employer-skills regarding, 71–72; diet for, 64, 73; drudgery and long hours work of, 73; hiring registries as source for, 72–73; housewife's options for improving lot of, 74; informal searches to hire, 72; interview of prospective, 73; lack of bedroom comforts for, 73; new middle-class attitudes required of, 74; priority need at hiring of first, 71; private registries as source for hiring, 72–73; reasons for departure of, 75; reasons for friction between housewife and, 74–75; wages of, 73–74; working conditions as compared to other options of, 74, 79 n.16
"The Servant Problem": acquiring an efficient house as solution to, 79; acquiring mechanical devices as solution to, 79; economics as cause of, 79; housewife's need to see domestic's point of view in solving, 74; ; simplification of household chores as solution to, 79; stress to housewife caused by, 71
Servants. *See* Cook, employed; Nursemaid; Servant, general
Sewing machine, domestic: advantage to older matron of, 188; dressmaker's use of, 38; hire-purchase plan of, 67; housewife's use of, 38; labor-saving and money-saving features of, 66; multiple uses of,

66–67; importance of, 66; professional competence developed on, 68; range of prices of, 67; time saving aspect of, 67; young girl use (mid-1800) of, 8
Sewing machine, industrial, 66
Sholes, Christopher, 175
Shoolbred's department store, 163
Shop assistants, employment of women as, 176
Shopping: Christmas, 130; MCMW's leisure activity of choice, 159–67; young girl's experience (mid-1800) of, 160
Shops, pre-1875. *See* Retail shop, traditional
Singer, Isaac, 66
Skin problems, 36–37
Small pox. *See* Disease, childhood
Swimming, seashore activity of, 132–33
Social activities, young women: 129–30; mixed-sex gatherings (mid-1800s), 9; mother's role in arranging, 9, 10, 130, 185–86
Social activities for children, 129
Social functions, adult: business gatherings for spouse as, 133–36; cost considerations of, 133; dinner parties as, 134–35; dinners with friends in city as, 136–37; holidays abroad, 137; musical evenings as, 135–36; ritual of dinner as, 134–135; theatre going with friends as, 136
Social functions, family: Christmas holiday as, 130; matron's role in arranging, 129, 130; seashore holiday as, 130–33
Spons' Household Manual, marketing advice in, 61
Sports: archery, croquet, tennis, and golf as examples of middle-class, 153; mixed social activity (mid-1800s) of, 9–10; older woman's limited interest in, 153
Spot-cleaning of unwashables, 55, 57 n.30
Spouse of MCMW: character of, 25–26; health of, 25; occupation of, 26
Starley, J. K., 153
Stockwell, 22
Street improvements, 173
Street lighting, gas, 16
Streets, cleaning of, 18, 19
Suburbs: attractions and development of, 21; liabilities of, 21; methods used to choose appropriate, 22; segregated occupational character of, 21; semblance of semi-rural existence in, 21
Surgery, female-related, 102
Swan, Joseph Wilson, 173

Tax returns: lack of class specific data in, 11 n.12; lack of income/occupation correlation data in, 5

Tea (the meal), 65
Techniques of selling, new: 82–83, 162. *See also* Department stores
Telegraph, 16–17; later decreased use of, 175
Telephone, 175
Telephone operators, jobs for young women as, 155
Terrace housing, structure of, 27; suburban, 21
Theatre, 136
"Theatrical purpose" use: domestic manual advice on lip coloring and rouge products for, 36–37
Thomas, W. F., 67
"Tiny waist" fashion, 41–42
Toiletries, availability of brand name, 37
Toilets, flushing, 32, 183
Tottenham, 22
Tottenham Court Road, 31
Toys of childhood, 122, 123
Tradesmen, city, suburban housing for, 22
Traffic, 17, 173
Traffic noise, 19
Trams, 16, 173
Trams, cable-hauled, 173
Treatise on Indigence, reliability of 1803 study acknowledged, 11 n.13
"Trial and Error" servant recruiting method, 73
Tricycle, use by matron of, 152
Typewriter, 175–76
Type-writers, office jobs for young women as, 155

Underground railway system, 16
United States, use of electric trolley in, 173
United Telephone Company, 17
"The Universal Provider." *See* Whiteley's Department Store
Upper-class women: charity activities of, 144–45; interest in mechanical labor-savings devices by, 176; monopoly of governesses by, 12 n.24; municipal pollution complaints from, 20
Upper-middle-class, use of governesses by, 7

Vaccination, 113
Vaginal pessary, sponge and syringe, 100
Vendors, 49
Victoria, Queen, 35, 172, 179
"The Victorian Sabbath," 142
Villas, suburban, 21
Vitamins, lack of knowledge about, 62

Walthamstow, 22
Walsh, John, 84
Ward & Lock's Home Book, advice on childhood ailments in, 113–14; beauty advice in, 36. *See also* Domestic manuals
"Washing dolly," 53–54
Washing machine, unavailability of electric, 183
Water distribution to homes, 29, 176–77

Waterloo, 16
"Watteau" back of tea gown, 40
Westminster Abbey, 15
Westminster Bridge, 16
Whiteley's Department Store, description of, 159–60; catering service ("hire & exhibitions") at, 167; goods (china, furniture, gentlemen's outfitting, glass, ladies' clothing, stationery) offered at, 159; services (gentlemen's tailoring, banking, dry cleaning, refreshment rooms, ticket agencies) at, 159
W. H. Smith bookstalls, 151
The Wife's Handbook, 100

Woman at Home, 150
Women, unescorted middle-class in London: hansom cabs for, 155; lack of eating places for, 154; limited number of "comfort stations" for, 155; male adjustments to, 154; public surface transport available for, 155; underground railways, time of day limitations for, 55
Women's magazines, domestic advice in. *See* Domestic manuals
World of Fashion, 67

Young girl. *See* Girl, young

Zoological Gardens, 15

About the Author

YAFFA CLAIRE DRAZNIN is a Visiting Scholar in the History Department at the University of Chicago. She is an independent British Victorian scholar, who returned to academia after 25 years as a published author and editor.

**Recent Titles in
Contributions in Women's Studies**

Untying the Tongue: Gender, Power, and the Word
Linda Longmire and Lisa Merrill, editors

Scheherazade's Sisters: Trickster Heroines and Their Stories in World Literature
Marilyn Jurich

Gender and Genre in Gertrude Stein
Franziska Gygax

Rewriting the Word: American Women Writers and the Bible
Amy Benson Brown

Ethnicity and Gender in the Barsetshire Novels of Angela Thirkell
Penelope Fritzer

Women of Courage: Jewish and Italian Immigrant Women in New York
Rose Laub Coser, Laura S. Anker, and Andrew J. Perrin

Contemporary Irish Women Poets: Some Male Perspectives
Alexander G. Gonzalez

Queer Poetics: Five Modernist Women Writers
Mary E. Galvin

White Women Writing White: H.D., Elizabeth Bishop, Sylvia Plath, and Whiteness
Renée R. Curry

The Foreign Woman in British Literature: Exotics, Aliens, and Outsiders
Marilyn Demarest Button and Toni Reed, editors

Embracing Space: Spatial Metaphors in Feminist Discourse
Kerstin W. Shands

On Top of the World: Women's Political Leadership in Scandinavia and Beyond
Bruce O. Solheim